This book is a
gift for you.
Yes, you !!.
I hope you
enjoy and we
are to
you.

D1106078

CONTENTS

YOU'RE WELCOME

◆ ◆ ◆

Capitalize on My Mental Breakdown to Improve Every Aspect of Your Physical, Cognitive, and Emotional Wellbeing

1ˢᵗ Edition, 1ˢᵗ printing 2021

ISBN: 978-1-7371732-1-2

DEDICATION

To my family, friends, classmates, coaches, teachers, and anyone who has had a positive and encouraging voice in my life. I am blessed to be surrounded and supported by such exceptional people. I also want to dedicate this book to David Bolger. You always believed in me and supported me in all my crazy endeavors. I would not be the woman I am today without having met you.

"Life is either a daring adventure or nothing at all." -Helen Keller

INTRODUCTION

August 15, 2019 - Bangalore, India

*"The only real mistake is the one from which
we learn nothing."* - Henry Ford

It's a blistering August day in Bangalore, India. I'm lounging by the pool outside my cottage and there is not a single soul to be seen, save two cows and an adorable monkey. I could not be any more relaxed, having just spent the entire week technology-free while indulging in endless yoga sessions and ancient Ayurveda treatments at the Shreya Yoga Retreat. I've just opened my laptop for the first time in seven days to confirm my flight, and out of nowhere I suddenly feel a strong urge to clean up my hard drive. Halfway through this tedious task, I happen upon a project file I had started several years ago and had all but forgotten, this book.

I originally archived these pages because I felt that writing, or typing out words, was my own form of cathartic release... and besides, who the heck would honestly want to read what I had written? Yet as I look around my cottage at the fifteen books that I've brought with me on this holiday, I immediately recognize the power and influence these authors wield in their ability to share their personal journeys. Some penned their stories to entertain, others aimed to enlighten, and others took me on an adventure. Each and every one of these books has provided me with something — whether it be education, advice, insight, hope — that has deeply inspired me to share my story with you.

I must admit that the thought of publishing this book is terrifying. To me, it feels like the equivalent of standing naked in front of the world with all my flaws exposed, not actually wanting anyone to look, yet somehow hoping at least one person glances my way with interest. It's been an uncomfortable process that has made me feel more vulnerable than I have ever felt in my entire life. That being said, I have persisted in sharing my story, because I believe that my knowledge and insights have the ability to help anyone out there who might be suffering, or just simply looking for more happiness, health, and joy in their life.

This is the story of how I experienced a total mental breakdown during a romantic vacation in Santorini, Greece: I was so tired, stressed, and out of tune physically that my body literally just broke. After this breakdown, I decided I could no longer sustain my current lifestyle marked by utter exhaustion and fatigue-plagued decisions, so I decided to wipe my brain clean and for lack of better words start from scratch at the ripe young age of 30ish.

I begin with an assessment of mental and physical health, and will touch on the key components of self-care: nutrition, exercise, sleep, morning routines, and mindfulness. Then I shift my focus to evaluating emotional health and discuss how one can establish and maintain healthy relationships with family, friends, coworkers and most importantly, yourself. Finally, I dive into deeper-level thinking and take readers on an adventure around Europe. I will share how I became a human guinea pig subjecting myself to experimental treatments such as sensory deprivation chambers and brain mapping, not to mention three long, painful trips to plant medicine ceremonies in England.

Additionally, I have added multiple life hacks and creative ways for readers to decrease daily stress and improve cognitive performance. I want to stress that you could spend an entire lifetime examining each of the topics I discuss in this book. However my objective is to just get you thinking about areas of your life that you may want to improve and to provide a starting point for pursuing that improvement. Although I think that it is important to understand some of the science in order to assign meaning to these concepts, I have purposely kept the chapters short and the scientific jargon to a bare minimum while still providing my honest opinion on these tools and experiences. Additionally, I include recommendations of who might best benefit from utilizing each of these individual options. One might also notice that certain concepts are repeated several times throughout the book. This is done intentionally because I am working to rewire the subconscious, thus consistency and repetition are key.

I truly believe that my breakdown was a blessing, and it has inspired me to commit to a lifetime of learning and service to help others avoid some of the pain and self-inflicted suffering that I endured for decades. My current academic background is rooted in human physiology, bioenergetics and public health, and my future plans include earning my PhD in Neuroscience. I currently work as a NeuroCoach and I teach my clients how to approach problem solving, anxiety, and emotions from a state of mindful awareness.

When I am working with a client who seems to be searching for a quick fix to a complex problem, he or she often expresses disappointment upon hearing my answers. There is no such thing as a magic pill or "one-size-fits-all" solution to any problem, be it a physical, mental or emotional one. Any doctor, author, coach or trainer that sells you on a panacea is not being honest with you. We are infinitely different, divine, unique individuals and each one of our bodies and minds will respond differently to different interventions. It is your own responsibility to understand your body, your mind, and your goals for your unique situation.

It took me a mental breakdown, thousands of dollars and a decade of intense trial and error for me to acquire this knowledge. The goal of this book is not only to share this journey but to provide you, the reader, with tools and resources to improve physical, cognitive, and emotional wellbeing. I'd also like to suggest that you listen to your intuition when reading this book. You don't have to read this book — or any book for that matter — from front to back. Think of this book as a toolkit: you may be fond of some of the tools and flat-out despise others. Some readers may want to learn more about the backstory of my breakdown, while others could care less and want to skip straight to the chapter on plant medicines. Trust me when I say that I won't be offended — this book is more about YOU the reader and what YOU can apply to your own life. I now stand naked before your eyes baring my body and soul, with the sincere hope that my personal journey inspires you to be a curious scientist experimenting and tinkering to achieve optimal happiness in your life.

PART ONE:
BREAKDOWN

1 SANTORINI, GREECE

"If you do not make time for your wellness, you will be forced to make time for your illness." -Unknown

The Greek island of Santorini is considered to be one of the most romantic places on earth due to its azure-colored Aegean Sea backdrop and its flawless sunsets. Photographs do not do it any justice — it is even more lovely in person, with the endless blue-domed roofs, stone-white buildings set against the vibrant glistening ocean. It was unlike anything I had ever seen before in my life... and of all places, it would end up being the location of my mental breakdown.

Up to this point in my life, things had been chaotic to say the least. I was spending my weekdays working at a challenging hospital assignment in Naples, Italy; on weekends, I often found myself jaunting off to exotic locations with my new boytoy from Sicily, whom I will refer to as K. K was exactly what I thought I needed in my life — I had not had a boyfriend since my divorce several years prior and I was naturally craving a bit of male attention. It seems almost comical for a Pittsburgh girl from a lower-middle class family to tell such a story, but I met K while staying in a chateau in St. Anton, Austria for a ski vacation. When we first met, I didn't give him the time of day since he was a good decade younger than me. Yet he remained quite persistent, so I reluctantly agreed to rendezvous after our ski vacation, and we eventually began dating and continued to date several months later.

Coordinating schedules with K was challenging because I lived on the mainland and he lived off the coast of Italy in Sicily, thus we could only see each other on the weekends. He was incredibly sweet and would plan these amazing trips where the only thing I would need to do was physically show up. We traveled to the Amalfi Coast, Athens, Munich, and we even toured the Neuschwanstein Castle that served as the inspiration for Disneyland's Sleeping Beauty castle. I was living a modern-day European fairy tale... which begs the question: how did my fairy tale take such an abrupt turn and become a nightmare with a dark ending?

On the outside, things appeared normal, even exemplary: I had been working in Italy for the past year and half and traveling the world while finishing my second master's degree from a world-renowned university. On the inside however I was crumbling, battling anxiety, depression, insomnia and frequent panic attacks. I was already starting to fall apart slowly, but little did I realize that my entire life was about to rapidly unravel in front of me.

In reality I was burning the candle on both ends. My current job assignment required me to work 60-plus hours a week and my challenging masters program required me to scramble to dedicate every free moment to attending classes and finishing homework assignments. Then, on Friday nights I would literally run from work straight to the airport to fly and meet up with K. I was subsisting on very little sleep, and I would sometimes roll over from one workday into the next without going to bed.

During this hectic period, I never once took a moment to ask myself if I was happy, tired, hungry or even excited about my life. Being the one neighborhood kid who had her first jobs at age 10 (assistant dog groomer and papergirl) and then the college student who worked three jobs while in school (plasma donor, professional notetaker, and manager of the student newspaper's business division), I was ingrained with the mantra that if you wanted something you had to work hard for it. Growing up, money was tight in my family and there always seemed to be a shortage of solid money-making opportunities on the horizon. I had never even taken a flight until I was in my 20s, thus jaunting around Europe every weekend was every bit as gratifying to my current self as it was preposterous to my younger self. Surely I could not be faulted for wanting to take advantage of every opportunity of my dreams while those opportunities lasted.

In addition to the stress of work and school, I also had well-meaning friends that began to question my relationship with K. They were most likely the questions you ask any single woman who dates a man who is significantly younger. Where was it going? Was he really serious about me? How did I know he wasn't seeing someone else? Wasn't I a little too old to be with him? To be honest, these thoughts never crossed my mind prior to my friends' inquiries, but once that seed was planted it was very hard to remove given my unstable mental and emotional state. That's when the self-doubt, worry, anxiety and chaos constantly being expressed by my inner voice began to take over. At first, I tried to continue my everyday life as I always had, smiling on the outside while falling apart on the inside and trying my damnedest to ignore that nagging voice in my head that was growing louder and louder.

Now, back to our regularly scheduled program: my breakdown. It was Friday night, I had only had eight hours of sleep the entire week, and once again I found myself running straight from work to the airport to board a plane for Athens, Greece to rendezvous with K. I was beyond exhausted, I felt physically and mentally horrible, had a loud ringing in my ears, a brick in my stomach, and now — thanks to my friends — my worries about the authenticity of my relationship with K were spinning full circle in my head. But of course I still got on that plane — After all, I was obligated, right? When I landed, K informed me that he had planned a special surprise where we would be heading to Santorini the next morning and we needed to be up at the crack of dawn. I was already exhausted, I couldn't think clearly, my head was pounding and my thoughts raced, but I sucked it up and gratefully thanked him. This was a once in a lifetime opportunity — lower-class girls from Pittsburgh steel and coal country just didn't get to do things like this. I got up early and forced a smile, but somewhere in the back of my mind I had the lingering feeling that today was going to be different.

Due to my extreme mental and physical fatigue, I was entirely incapable of enjoying myself or making good decisions. So, what did I do when we arrived in Santorini, the most romantic place on earth? Well, I proceeded to get really, really, REALLY drunk that afternoon at a wine tasting. And then, out of nowhere, I just cracked... and I started to release all the toxic shit that had been building inside of me for decades. As I reflect back on that day, my hands start to shake because it is still so painful to think about. Inebriated, at my wit's end, and sans inhibitions, I just let the verbal vomit flow, and it was projectile. It flowed for hours, sloppily spewing forth into the open for all to witness. "I hate my job." "My life sucks." "I was destined for unhappiness because I had a bad childhood." I will never be normal." "Everyone is against me and conspiring to make my life miserable." My tirade continued for eight straight hours, moving from the wine tasting to the bus ride home to our hasty dinner to the latest of hours in our hotel suite. It was like a demon had possessed my body for a day, and I could just not bring myself under control.

At long last, my rage began to dissipate and I eventually drifted off to sleep. When I woke up the next day, I was filled with so many emotions that I wanted to crawl out of my skin and start screaming. But K was a very calm person, and he was determined to enjoy the remainder of our trip. He took me hiking to see one of Santorini's world-renowned sunsets, and at our dinner he literally got down on his knees — not to propose (whew!), but to ever so sweetly change my shoes. It was incredibly thoughtful and kind, particularly after I had just put him through 24 hours of hell.

Being the totally rational person that I was, I did what I thought was right: I broke up with him on the flight home from Greece.

Innately, I knew for the first time in my life that I needed to take some time alone to deal with this mess of a life that I had somehow created. I returned home to Italy feeling deflated and defeated, and I told myself that my mental breakdown must have happened for a very specific reason. I believed that this experience of hitting rock-bottom and total exhaustion could be used as an opportunity to reevaluate my life, relationships, self-care, emotional well-being, values and goals. I was sick of listening to everyone else tell me who I was and what I needed to be, because clearly that was not working and I could not keep living as I had.

Before my big breakdown, I believed myself to be an invincible robot, and I treated my body like a machine. In fact, a few years earlier I underwent not one but two heart surgeries to correct a congenital heart condition. Nevertheless, I still abused my body in every way shape and form in the interest of keeping myself going. I was taking a pill to give me energy in the morning, another one to help me sleep, and tons of caffeine in between to keep me chugging along. I hardly ever stopped to rest or ask myself if I actually enjoyed what I was doing; I never asked myself if I loved — or even liked — my life, job, relationships, friends, etc. If you asked me why I got out of the bed in the morning and what inspired me, I would not have had an answer. I was just flying on autopilot with my head in the clouds until my body screamed "Mayday" and crash-landed.

It has taken me several years of self-reflection, investigation, and trial-and-error tinkering, but I now understand that I lacked basic self-care and was totally out of touch with my body's physical, mental and emotional needs. In the following section I will cover, on a very basic level, the areas of self-care that with more focus applied could have helped to prevent my breakdown. These are foundational pillars that one can use to restructure the way you nurture your mind and body and to move towards living your best life.

2 NUTRITION

"Let food be thy medicine, and let medicine be thy food." -Hippocrates

At the point of my breakdown, I was eating nothing but takeout and whatever I could find in the vending machines at the hospital where I worked. I had actually convinced myself that I didn't have time to sit down and eat a healthy meal, so I would eat whatever was most convenient. Then I would scarf the entire thing down — never once stopping to savor or enjoy what I was eating, which led to chronic bouts of constipation, indigestion, heartburn and a nagging feeling like there was a brick in my stomach. My poor food choices combined with mindless eating habits were taking their toll on my already exhausted and run-down body. After years of this self-abuse, I decided to press the reset button starting with an in-depth analysis on the science of nutrition.

Early on in my analysis, I discovered an inspirational quote that has been forever ingrained into my memory: "Let food be thy medicine, and let medicine be thy food." This statement comes from Hippocrates, a pioneer of medicine who lived in Ancient Greece over 2,000 years ago. Hippocrates — yes, the one who authored the ubiquitous oath of medicine that all doctors and nurses recite — was one of the first practitioners to challenge the ancient notion that disease was a punishment from the gods. An intelligent man, Hippocrates understood that human bodies and minds responded acutely to the types of food we consume, and that many foods could work as medicine — or in my specific case, as poison.

Hippocrates introduced his patients to the idea that food affects our holistic health, and thousands of years later, researchers continue to investigate the significance of this relationship. In a recent *Harvard Medical School* article, scientists explain that our brains are constantly operating and require a substantial amount of energy to function properly.[1] And in alignment with Hippocrates, they agree that what you eat affects the structure of your brain and the quality of your mood. Your brain functions best when fueled with high-quality, nutrient-dense foods that protect it from oxidative stress. In contrast, your brain can be damaged by low-premium fuel such as processed or refined foods. Several studies have also shown a correlation between refined sugars and impaired brain function, including the promotion of mood disorders like depression.[2]

There is currently a wealth of conflicting nutritional advice and misinformation surrounding healthy eating. One of my favorite examples of this is the endless barrage of advertisements that were shown during the Saturday morning cartoons of my childhood. Cereal commercials would boast of scientific studies that "proved" breakfast was the most important meal because without it we wouldn't have the energy to tackle the day. The truth is that these studies were funded by companies like Kellogg's and Quaker Oats, who is owned by Pepsi, a company whose high-fructose corn syrup products dominate our grocery stores. (Side note: if you want to read something even more shocking about nutrition, run a web search on the phrase "Why was Kellogg's invented?")

To make matters worse, there are an endless number of "experts" promoting an endless parade of newfangled diets: the low-carb diet, the grapefruit diet, the blood type diet, the baby food diet, the magnetic diet, the zen diet, the cotton ball diet, and yes even the tapeworm diet. Even my own mother once called to inform me that she was on a diet where she eliminated lettuce, because one of these diet gurus had convinced her it was making her fat! As someone who has studied metabolism at a molecular level, that type of misguided statement drove me up the wall.

I would be ecstatic if human society could just toss the word "diet" into the trash: this singular word has become practically inseparable in most people's minds from the fad and quick-fix approaches that typically produce only short-term benefits. Instead, you should be working to incorporate small changes to your daily regimen as opposed to attempting extreme changes once or twice a year. Research strongly suggests that crash diets are useless, because often when one forces rapid weight loss upon himself or herself, the weight will eventually return. The TV show *The Biggest Loser* is the perfect example: an article published in the research journal *Obesity* shows that six years after the competition, a majority of participants gained back approximately 70% of their original weight, implying that extreme weight loss is not sustainable long-term.[3]

Of course, there is also a strong psychological component to eating. Before you take that next bite, ask yourself a few questions: 1) Does this actually taste good, or am I eating it out of habit? 2) Am I genuinely hungry, or am I just eating because I am stressed? 3) Am I actually tasting this food, or am I just wolfing it down because I don't want to deal with some uncomfortable emotion? Now, let's follow these questions with an experiment. The next time you are about to eat take pause, put down your phone, turn off the TV, and remove any extraneous distractions. Then before you take that first bite, take a deep breath and take the time to savor what you eat. Finally, take careful note of how you feel an hour after eating. Are you energized, exhausted, bloated, or still hungry? Over time, with patience and self-observation, you will come around to hearing and learning what your body needs.

My personal nutritional program includes intermittent fasting during the week and indulging on the weekends. Research shows that the benefits of periodic fasting include reduced inflammation, improved blood pressure, lower triglycerides and choles-terol levels, and prevention of neurodegenerative disorders but I personally love that it provides me with mental clarity and stamina.[4] For my fast, I have an eating window from 12pm-8pm Monday through Thursday during which I utilize several types of flexible fasting routines incorporating consumption of less than 600 calories a day, liquid diets, and food-free days. To learn about intermittent fasting and programs that might work for your per-sonal routine, I recommend reading *The Ultimate Guide to Fasting* by Smart Nourishment. And if you would like to experiment with a simple five-day low-calorie fasting program, I'd suggest the fast-ing-mimicking program by Prolon®. An item of note concerning the program: since this is an extended low-calorie diet, you will have to conserve your energy, so working out while on this regi-men is not recommended.

In addition to engaging in fasting, I also eat clean, unprocessed foods such as fruits, vegetables, and lean meats, with a focus on nutrient-dense foods that boost immune function like citrus fruits, garlic, turmeric and ginger. I also drink plenty of vegetable and fruit smoothies, and if I feel like my diet needs an extra boost I add superfood and plant protein powders (Your Super® is my fa-vorite brand). One culture I deeply admire because of its emphasis on clean eating is the Japanese. The majority of their foods come from the earth, are not overprocessed and thus stripped of their key nutrients, and have an abundance of nutritious properties. To learn more about the benefits of the Japanese diet, I highly recom-mend the book *Japanese Foods that Heal: Using Traditional Japanese Ingredients to Promote Health, Longevity, & Well-Being* by Jon and Jan Belleme.

Caffeinated drinks are also a staple in my life. I understand that there is substantial controversy around the health benefits of coffee, but my belief is that it is not inherently bad and what you add to your coffee — creamers, synthetic sweeteners, whipped cream, for example — is what can turn it toxic. Coffee, and more specifically caffeine, helps to burn fat and stimulates cognition, focus, and release of dopamine, a key neurotransmitter for motivation. Occasionally I like to mix it up and substitute my coffee with Kin Euphorics, a sparkling drink made from adaptogens, nootropics and botanicals, which are fancy words for herbs, roots, and fungi that help the body return to homeostasis. Some people drink Kin as a substitute for alcohol, but I find that it has a bubbly refreshing taste that gives me the perfect midday pick-me-up when coffee simply won't do the job. I also love Runa® energy drinks made from the guayusa leaf — I find they provide me mental clarity and focus without the jitters.

If you want to improve your diet but feel confused and overwhelmed, then use the KISS method and keep it simple. Start by evaluating the types of food that you consume on a daily basis and then ask yourself: Is this processed? Did this come directly from the earth? Is sugar or high-fructose corn syrup one of the first few ingredients? Food labels list ingredients in order of quantity, so if one of the first five ingredients is sugar or high-fructose corn syrup you should strongly resist the urge to take that first bite or sip.

As for breakfast, there is no research proving that skipping this meal leads to weight gain, lack of energy or any other health issue. In fact, not eating breakfast actually helps you to burn fat faster. Add a cup of black coffee and a workout in there before you eat and your body becomes a fat burning machine. Again, keep to the KISS method: if you wake up hungry, eat and if not, don't.

When it comes to that next meal, I'd like you to keep the great Hippocrates in mind. Remember that a daily diet heavy in processed and high-sugar foods can lead to obesity, type 2 diabetes, anxiety, depression and a plethora of additional ailments, so strive to make healthy choices with the flexibility to indulge when your body is craving something like chocolate or red wine. Also, take a moment to slow down and assess your mental state before taking that first bite, take the time to savor your food, and make note of how you feel an hour after you eat.

Choose a well-balanced diet and eating plan — one that you enjoy, that works for your daily and weekly schedule, and that is sustainable over the long-term. Reminder: there is no "one-size-fits-all" diet for everyone. Your daily diet should be something that is unique to you, your metabolism, your body type, your insulin sensitivity and your daily caloric needs. If you don't know the answers to these questions, then you should reach out to a nutritionist, dietician, or other health professional.

Now go grab a glass of red wine and get to work!

3 EXERCISE

"Food is the most widely abused anti-anxiety drug in America, and exercise is the most potent yet underutilized antidepressant." -Bill Phillips

Next to nutrition, I believe the most important component of self-care is exercise, because it will also affect every aspect of your physical and mental health. The physical benefits of exercise are plentiful and include weight loss, longevity, increased bone mass density and decreased cancer risk. Psychologically speaking, exercise has been shown to improve cognitive function and self-esteem and to decrease anxiety and depression.[5]

If the health benefits aren't enough motivation and you are still struggling to begin or maintain a regular exercise routine, I'd like to suggest that you get creative. First, identify an activity that you enjoy doing and make sure that this activity can be incorporated into a sustainable routine. If you wake up and dread having to work out, you need to find a different exercise program that motivates and inspires you to start moving. It can be anything that gets your heart pumping such as tai chi, boxing, dancing or even rollerblading. And don't cast the blame upon lack of time or money for not engaging in exercise. You can get outside for free, and the internet provides millions of free workout videos that you can do in the comfort of your home.

In the previous chapter, I touched upon the massive weight gain reported from participants on *The Biggest Loser* competition show. This was due in part to the unsustainability of their extreme workout regimes. When designing your individual exercise program, you should include activities that you can easily incorporate into your life over the long term. And if time is truly an issue, you only need 15 minutes. Believe it or not, just 15 minutes of exercise will provide you with all the physical and mental benefits I have listed above. And as many individuals discover soon after embarking on their journey, you may only initially aim for 15 minutes of exercise yet with continued commitment soon find yourself working out longer and longer with each passing session.

Fortunately, lack of exercise has never been an issue for me. As a child I was a competitive year-round swimmer, so the majority of my childhood and teens consisted of 4am wake up calls, three swim workouts a day, and lots of cross-training. I am lucky because that same workout discipline is now ingrained in my blood and working out is just a daily habit I perform with little issue, like brushing my teeth. Also, if I go two or three consecutive days without working out, I can feel the stress and anxiety monsters creeping into my head that tell me it's time to get off my couch and engage in physical activity.

But let's say that you are new to working out and don't know where to start. If you are on a budget, then experiment with taking classes at your local YMCA, walking outdoors, or going directly to YouTube and checking out my workout channel playlist. What if you already have an established workout routine and are looking for something a little more intense or challenging? Then I'd ask you if you would rather sprint one mile or slowly jog five miles. This simple question can help you determine your dominant muscle fiber type, and thus the types of workouts you might enjoy most.

Your body is composed of two types of muscle fibers: slow-twitch (type I) and fast-twitch (type II). Slow-twitch fibers support long distance endurance activities; fast-twitch fibers are utilized for quick powerful movements like weightlifting and sprinting. In most individuals, one type of fiber is dominant to the other and it's helpful to understand your muscle fiber type when designing your workouts. Personally, the thought of sprinting a mile makes me want to vomit, but that's because my dominant muscle fiber type is slow-twitch (type I). This means that my body prefers long, slow aerobic workouts and to be honest, I love and look forward to them.

I also approach exercise as a moving meditation which provides me with mental clarity, focus, insights and creative problem solving. When I am struggling with a complex problem or challenging decision, I plan a long workout that might include hours of yoga or cycling. I used to compete in endurance sports and therefore am confident my body can physically handle these extended sessions, therefore these workouts become more of a mental challenge for me. The workouts typically begin with racing thoughts, a negative attitude, or anxiety over a decision, so I start by taking a deep breath and reminding myself to be present. Then when I notice my mind starts to wander or make excuses as to why I should stop, I simply stop and take another deep breath. This may continue for an hour or so, but if I can totally immerse myself in what the instructor is saying or the music in the room, something magical will begin to happen.

As long as I remain present, my inner thoughts will eventually subside and my body will begin to move automatically without pain or stress. Then without any conscious effort, a solution or insight will come to mind like magic. We will get more into the brain science behind this in a later chapter, but for now think of it as a "shower thought" — you know, the kind of thought that appears out of nowhere while you are taking a shower and often leads to an epiphany. An added bonus is that during and after workouts, feelings of anxiety or depression often dissipate, replaced by feelings of euphoria and satisfied accomplishment. Science ties this to the body's release of endorphins during prolonged periods of exercise — the well-publicized "runner's high." These feel-good chemicals are not unique to running — you can obtain this feeling of physical and mental bliss from any form of exercise.

My personal approach is to plan my workouts while planning my weekly work schedule each Sunday. I look for windows of one to two free hours in my day and start getting creative. I personally think variety is the key to sustainability, and I try to mix it up. I prefer yoga, cycling, dance, barre or at-home workouts. When working out at home I turn to two of my favorite YouTube channels, POPSUGAR Fitness and Pamela Reif. These two channels alone offer thousands of free at-home workout videos that are updated weekly and consist of everything from high-intensity interval training to yoga and everything in-between. I am also a fan of Tracy Anderson's workouts because her dance-inspired routines focus on working smaller muscle groups that traditional exercises do not target. This is important if you are not looking to bulk up or gain significant muscle mass but please note that you will have to invest in her DVDs or online training studio.

My final advice in this arena is just to get moving in any way, shape or form. Get inspired, find something you love doing, and commit to spending a few days every week improving your body and mind. Aim to alternate between workouts that focus on flexibility, muscular development, and cardiovascular activity. An example routine with ample variety is yoga for flexibility, weight training or weight-bearing exercises for muscular development, and some form of cardiovascular training which can include running, biking, or swimming. And when you feel exhausted, you should listen to your body and shut it down for rest, because this is a critical component of your routine that helps to rebuild your muscles and provide motivation for your next workout. If you need some encouragement or support, don't hesitate to reach out to friends and family or enroll in group fitness programs. I promise that you will begin to see improvements in both your mind and your body, and it will be well worth the initiative and effort.

4 SLEEP

"I love sleep, my life has a tendency to fall apart when I am awake." -Ernest Hemingway

If you're one of those people who lives by the mantra "I'll sleep when I'm dead!" then I can speak from first-hand experience that this approach might just kill you. Sleep is a critical factor of self-care that I myself had been ignoring for years. By disregarding my body's need to rest, I disrupted a number of physiological pathways responsible for immune function, cell repair and blood pressure normalization. And when I rolled over from one workday to the next without resting, I was risking my emotional and cognitive health while simultaneously increasing my susceptibility to depression and anxiety.[6]

If that alone isn't enough to scare you into recalibrating your lifestyle, also consider this: chronic lack of sleep will also take a toll on your physical appearance and accelerate the aging process. Sleeplessness results in increased levels of cortisol — the primary stress hormone — and the breakdown of skin collagen. Deep sleep is necessary for the release of growth hormone and losing sleep may result in weight gain because sleep loss stimulates appetite and cravings for high fat, high carbohydrate foods. And here's the final kicker: scientific studies have conclusively proven that prolonged sleep deprivation can kill you.[7]

There's no harm in taking the occasional sleeping pill to adjust to a new sleep schedule, but the continuous use of these medications can be detrimental. Research suggests that frequent use of sleeping pills causes subjects to skip the sleep cycle that produces restorative hormones and other aforementioned physiological benefits. In addition, sleeping pills have numerous negative side effects such as daytime drowsiness, difficulty concentrating, impaired memory, and severe allergic reactions; they are by no means an ideal long-term solution to resolving sleep issues.[8]

Sleep is a complex issue because individuals have varying levels of daily activity and different circadian rhythm cycles, thus requiring different amounts of sleep from person to person. Sleep is also challenging because while one can catch up on lost sleep, one cannot store excess sleep; as a result, one single sleepless night can prove to be detrimental. One simple rule of thumb is that if you need daily naps and feel noticeably exhausted throughout the day, you definitely need to get more rest.

Just like diet and exercise, the solution for a good night's rest will be unique to you. If lack of good sleep has been a chronic issue or you believe you have a sleep disorder, then please contact your physician. Otherwise, it's time to start playing scientist to determine what works best for you. I recommend beginning with sleep hygiene — an all-encompassing concept covering every aspect of your life that pertains to sleep. I've simplified sleep hygiene into three main categories: daily schedule, bedtime routine, and sleep environment.

There are multiple aspects of your daily routine that will affect your ability to sleep at night. You will want to observe and take into consideration the timing of your workouts, dinner, and your last caffeinated drink of the day. If you do any of these things too late in the day it can be over-stimulating and affect your body's ability to fall asleep. Another key factor is your sleep-wake cycle. If you are constantly getting up and going to bed at different times each day you are confusing your body, so it's best to set a schedule and stick to it. Additionally, the human psyche tends to function more efficiently through habit and association. Thus, your bedroom should only be used for two things: sleep and the other thing I won't mention but I'm confident you've already guessed. If you are using your bed to eat, watch TV, or hang out, then there is a higher likelihood that you may encounter trouble falling asleep at bedtime.

I begin my bedroom routine approximately one to two hours prior to going to sleep. This usually starts with me planning my schedule for the next day and powering down my TV, computer and any other electronic devices. If I know I have to work late, then I use my blue-light blocking glasses and a free app called f.lux®. I love f.lux® because it automatically adapts your computer display to the time of day or night by making it brighter during the day and dimming your screen at night.

Next, I turn to the kitchen to drink some chamomile or sleep tea and I also might add valerian root or melatonin. If I am feeling particularly stressed, I will consume a drink that is high in magnesium like Natural Vitality's CALM®. Magnesium is the fourth most abundant mineral in the human body, and most people consume much less than they need. According to an article published by the journal *Magnesium Research,* magnesium helps your body and brain to relax by activating the parasympathetic nervous system and by regulating key neurotransmitters and the melatonin, the hormone that guides sleep-wake cycles.[9]

When it's finally time for bed, I lower the thermostat because body temperature tends to lower when you go to sleep and then slowly rises, and I have woken up many mornings covered in sweat. My bedroom is stocked with bamboo bedding because it's breathable, soft, and keeps me cool throughout the night. I also use a sleep clock because it has a wind-down feature with a soft light that will slowly darken over the course of 5-60 minutes so I can crack a book, start to read and peacefully drift off to sleep. Another advantage of these clocks is that they also have a soft light and can produce natural noise to help you wake up gradually so that you aren't jolted awake the next morning.

Another key component of my sleep routine is peaceful scents. According to the *Journal of Medicine*, biologists believe that the effect of smell modulates behavior.[10] Certain scents trigger certain reactions, and our sense of smell is controlled by the same part of our brain that manages sleep. I personally love lavender and will either use a spray onto my pillow or a diffuser within my bedroom. Other popular calming scents include rose, geranium, jasmine and clary sage. You can also purchase scented eye pillows for the added benefit of blocking early morning light that might disturb your sleep.

There are literally thousands of books, devices, tools and techniques to help you sleep — smart pillows, sleep headphones, blackout curtains, mouth guards for night teeth grinders. One of my favorite books is Paul McKenna's *I Can Make You Sleep* which includes a sleep hypnosis download. Sleep hypnosis and sleep music have a very powerful, relaxing effect on me, so I have included sleep and powernap playlists on my YouTube Channel.

When I started to experiment with my own sleep routine, I tried something called David's Delight which you can find on Amazon. This is a funny-looking device that looks like it came right out of the 1980s and it utilizes brainwave entrainment to relax your brain into a restful state for sleep. It can also be used for mediation, concentration and relaxation. And despite the odd exterior and ridiculous name, I loved the product for its effectiveness. (Side note: I also went so far as to purchase an at-home transcranial direct-current stimulator or TDCS, which delivers a low direct current via electrodes placed on your head to create the same calming effects. This device actually lit my hair on fire while I was sleeping, so you might want to steer clear of this product!)

Finally, even if I have had the perfect bedtime routine but my daily worries are keeping me from resting, I spend a few moments reflecting on everything positive that I accomplished during the day and create a list of things for which I am grateful. And at all costs I avoid focusing on negativity or failure — research has shown that if you focus on the positives in your life before drifting off to sleep, your overall happiness and well-being will gradually improve.[11]

Once I figured out the factors that kept me up late and adjusted my bedtime routine, I have had far more restful nights than sleepless ones and it has definitely helped to improve my physical and mental health. Not every night is going to yield the perfect night's rest, but that's OK. This journey to find good sleep will truly be a drawn-out process of trial and error, so be patient with yourself. And again, if you think your sleeplessness is related to a medical condition, please reach out to your physician.

5 MORNING ROUTINE

*"To get up each morning with the resolve to be happy…
is to set our own conditions to the events of each day.
To do this is to condition circumstances instead of being
conditioned by them." -Ralph Waldo Emerson*

A s I begin this chapter, I want to acknowledge that some people have obligations that do not allow them the freedom and flexibility to design their ideal morning. If you are fortunate enough to have this leeway, then I would like to ask: What is the very first thing you do when you wake up?

If the answer is to look at your phone, then that is natural but it's also one of the worst things you can do for your brain and body. Our brains were designed to look for threats in our environment, and you subconsciously stimulate this innate threat response when you look at your phone first thing in the morning. Whether you realize it or not, you are immediately raising stress hormone levels and pushing your body into a state of fight-or-flight, which leads to you entering into your day from the worst mental state possible. This stress response was more useful in the days of early man when there was a snarling saber-toothed tiger standing above you when you woke up, but in today's world it's not as pertinent.

It is important to understand that your brain has been conditioned to immediately look for the negative in every situation. You are likely familiar with that inner voice that starts to chatter the moment you wake up, worrying you with all you need to accomplish today and regretting everything you did wrong yesterday. Once you grab your cell phone, you amplify that negative voice and put yourself into a state of stress instead of just simply allowing yourself a mindful moment to relax, clear your mind and wake up fully and efficiently.

I used to read my texts and work emails immediately upon waking, and I would be stressed from the second I woke up to the second I went to bed. And in retrospect, all of those things could have waited an hour or two. The next time you wake up and pick up your phone, I want you to have a mental picture of me smacking it right out of your hand — if I was there next to you, that's exactly what I would do.

Hypothetically, let's say that you ignored my advice: you just woke up and started checking emails, reading the news, or trolling Instagram because it's a necessary part of your morning and you absolutely have to see what your friends are eating for breakfast (my sarcastic tone is completely intentional and should be jumping off the page at you). Instead of priming your brain for you and your goals, your head is now in a tailspin thinking about everyone else. You have consciously allowed the outside world to hijack your thoughts, and your focus is now external versus internal.

We have a limited amount of cognitive capacity and thinking power each day before our brain becomes depleted of key neurotransmitters responsible for concentration and focus. I strongly urge you not to waste too much of your valuable brain power on Instagram. Of course I understand that it does feel good to scroll through social media — in fact, researchers have shown that the sound created by a new message in your inbox or a like on social media releases dopamine, that feel-good neurotransmitter that makes you feel rewarded. The brain naturally craves dopamine, and the more you give your brain its fix, the bigger the fix you need next time in order to get that same level of "feel-good" feeling.

Yes, social media works in the same neurochemical pathways as crack cocaine releasing massive amounts of serotonin and dopamine.[12] And, yes, the creators of social media are well aware of that fact... and yes, they love that you wake up and check your phone or they would be out of business. Numerous research studies have been conducted to study the relationship between online networking and mental health, and the results are grim: prolonged use of social networking sites can lead to depression, low self-esteem, and they can promote narcissistic and/or addictive behaviors.[13]

I know subject matter gurus and successful businesspeople who have meticulously detailed two-hour morning routines, but that is a bit excessive and isn't actually ideal for the rest of us. If you only have twenty minutes, then try this: wake up and do not immediately check your phone. Take a few minutes to shut off your inner voice if it is focused on something negative, take a few slow, deep breaths. Tell the right hemisphere of your brain — the half focused on fear and dwelling on the past — to shut up. In all seriousness, say the words "SHUT UP!" out loud and with enthusiasm. I love and highly recommend this hack — without fail it helps me to silence those negative thoughts and reminds me that today is a new day.

If you have the time, I also encourage a quick meditation or body scan to see which areas of your body are tight or in pain. Just a few minutes of morning stretching and deep breathing can help keep you relaxed during your daily routine. Additionally, light morning exercise or a brisk walk in nature is an excellent idea. And before you open the newspaper, turn on the phone or pet and feed your furry friend, ask yourself: What is it that I want to accomplish today? What kind of day do I want to have? Rushed and stressed, or relaxed and efficient? Intention, especially first thing in the morning, is very powerful and it helps to start your day off on a positive note.

Here is a typical morning in the life of Rachel. First, I sit up in my bed, tell my right-side brain to shut up, and take a few slow stretches. Then I grab one of my favorite motivational books and simply read one page because your subconscious is highly impressionable right before you fall asleep and also immediately when you wake up. Thus, these are the ideal times to fill your head with positive thoughts, future goals and a solid intention for the day. I also watch a 10-minute MindMovie® (I will talk about this more later in the book) which is a video where you can create your ideal life. Think of a video vision board with music.

Then I head to the kitchen to prime my immune system while listening to motivational speeches on YouTube. I start with a shot of apple cider vinegar because it wakes me up and provides beneficial antimicrobial, antioxidant and blood sugar stabilizing properties. Then I take a scoop of Morning Complete™ by ActivatedYou™ and add it to eight ounces of water. I absolutely love to drink this first thing in the morning because it's a combination of prebiotics, probiotics, and green superfoods that support digestion and provide energy for my busy days. Lastly I make my immune tea which consists of fresh lemon, lime, hot tea (I blend white, green, and oolong), turmeric, ashwagandha, chlorophyll, bacopa, oregano, iodine with kelp, and any other natural substances I feel like playing with that week. (You might be wondering how this tastes: not horrible, but not great. I just have to tell myself, this food is my medicine). After taking my tea, I am free to fill my head with email and news... but certainly not social media as I will save that for later.

Every time I veer from this routine and start my day off on the wrong foot, I always regret it. So start playing around with your morning routine, get creative, and let me know your insights and what works for you. I'd love to hear them all, but NOT until after you've finished your morning routine — only then can you turn on your phone, start your workday, and shoot me an email or direct message.

6 MINDFULNESS BREAKS

"Taking time to do nothing often brings everything into perspective." -Doe Zantamata

We are human beings, not human doings. Somewhere along life's journey you might have been brainwashed into thinking that to be successful, you need to be hyper-efficient and complete massive amounts of work each day. Often during those times when we aren't working, we still spend that time bragging about how busy we are at work. In fact, we are so busy and work so hard that by the end of the day — instead of working out, meditating, or spending time with family and friends — we are so drained that we plop in the front of the TV to binge watch the latest Netflix series until we pass out on the couch. Then we wake up the next day and repeat the cycle, endlessly running from task to task and never taking the time to appreciate the people around us or breathe in the present moment.

That previous paragraph described me perfectly, and I was a ticking time bomb. When I began my stressful job overseas, I behaved as my predecessors did. I performed, I came in early, I stayed late, and I did not stop for lunch or idle chit-chat. I had a large staff of Italians working for me, and every morning I walked into work with my head down, ran into my office and shut my door. When one of my staff wanted to make small talk about their vacation or child, I would have them walk with me on the way to my next meeting or I would half-listen and nod my head as I worked to finish some other task. I was never really engaged or listening because I had too much work to do and I viewed each minute in the office through myopic lens of completing one task quickly and efficiently so I could move on to the next.

Do you know what happened? My staff stopped working for me, because I was not likable nor had I earned their respect. In the Italian culture, relationships are crucial: you don't come to the office and immediately start working, you have a cafe and chat with your co-workers about the amazing pizza you ate last night and debate over how to make the best limoncello. Then through-out the day, you take several breaks to walk outside or visit friends in a different department. You take little moments to enjoy life and then you go back to your work, because that work isn't going anywhere.

Before I arrived at this new job, I was instructed that Italians were lazy and that they needed to be ruled with an iron first, but that was not the case and couldn't be further from the truth. Many Americans just did not fathom how much Italians value human connection. In Italian culture, you come to work to do your job and to socialize. You treat people with respect and you take the time to hear what they have to say. Italians did not take frequent breaks because they were lazy; they took them to energize and re-charge so that they would not burn out.

I cringe and I am ashamed of my professional behavior when I think back on those days. I dare not imagine what they thought of me at the time: an angry, sullen American woman who did noth-ing but work and only cared about herself. Reflecting back on this, I recognize that this job was extremely outside my comfort zone and I was simply struggling to survive. However, if I had just taken a second for myself to breathe and to get to know the people who worked for me on a deeper level — simply to walk outside with them or to sit down with them and have a proper lunch — we all would have been happier and much better off as colleagues. But I just couldn't, because I had to perform... I had to keep on keeping on.

Since then, I have come to the realization that the relationships one establishes with others are the most valuable commodities one can acquire, and in order for me to establish and nurture these high-value assets I needed to be present. One way I worked to change my mindset in order to become more present and more mindful of the people around me is by taking frequent mindfulness breaks.

Mindfulness breaks aid in concentration, problem solving, emotional regulation and communication, but they also serve another purpose. The hot new topic in neuroscience is brain network theory, which tells us that multiple brain regions — as opposed to single structures in the brain — work in tandem to perform different activities. The Central Executive Network (CEN), which is responsible for concentration, focused attention and goal-oriented decision making, can become depleted of key neurotransmitters necessary for focus; frequent breaks help to flush the brain of any stress chemicals and replenish these key neurotransmitters.[14] Put more simply, you can work longer, and with more cognitive power, if you take several breaks throughout the day.

Another quick and easy way to reset the CEN is by yawning. Try yawning very slowly several times and evaluate how you feel before and afterward. Don't worry if it feels forced or unnatural and you feel a bit silly at first — it will still work. Yawning is a thermoregulatory mechanism that has been shown to reduce stress and anxiety and prime your brain for concentration.[15] So the next time you are in class nodding off or a boss calls you out for not paying attention because you are yawning, feel free to defend yourself: you are just priming your CEN to focus on interesting subject matter, and your yawn should be taken as a compliment!

I strive to incorporate mindfulness into my daily routine, and it begins when I sit down at my desk each morning. I stop to take a few deep breaths before powering up my laptop and then I use a post-it note to write down two things: one positive manta and one expression of gratitude. Then I set my online mindfulness clock and program it to ring every 15 minutes. When the bell chimes I stop and listen for a full 60 seconds. I empty my mind, take a deep breath, yawn, and glance at my post-it note; immediately afterward I feel refreshed and ready to dive into my next task. Then every hour or so when my brain starts to feel mushy and sluggish, I stop working and get up from my desk for a longer break and possibly a walk outside. Once you start to incorporate mindfulness breaks into your routine, you start to become more attuned to when your body is asking for them.

Using a mindfulness clock also allows me to tap into two additional brain networks: the salience network and the default mode network. These two networks are responsible for imagination, mind wandering, insight, and intuition, and you can exploit them when you are totally immersed in the present moment. Recall the "shower thought" epiphanies I described in Chapter 2 — these "A-ha!" moments are the manifestation of these two networks functioning in synergy. Surprisingly, when you turn your attention away from a problem or task and do nothing, a large portion of your upper brain becomes active and this is when the magic happens. This is the reasoning behind why I use endurance exercise for problem solving. When you consciously enter a state of relaxed mindful awareness, you can ask your intuition for insights to creatively solve any problem.

If you have not yet made a conscious attempt to practice mindfulness, then I recommend beginning by utilizing a bell or setting a timer on your phone. If you are looking to improve your current mindfulness practice or want a more formal mindfulness training program, the Palouse Mindfulness website offers a free Mindfulness Based Stress Reduction course. You also might be wondering if and how meditation relates to mindfulness training. Meditation is the overarching practice used to train attention and awareness and to work towards a clear and emotionally calm state. Mediation can involve different techniques such as compassion, love, patience, or mindfulness. Mindfulness is the act of focusing on the present and rooting out overpowering emotions from the mind. Research shows that subjects who practice mindfulness have healthier glucose levels, improved focus, better self-control and sleep, and lowered anxiety and depression levels.[16,17] In my personal life, I practice shorter meditations (i.e., 10 minutes or less) right when I wake up or before I go to bed, and I actively work to be more mindful throughout the day. This routine works best for me, but you may want to experiment to find what is best for you and your daily routine.

For those readers wondering what eventually happened to my staff in Italy, I am happy to report that this chapter of my professional life had a happy ending. I experienced my mental breakdown halfway through my three-year assignment in Italy, which led me to begin incorporating mindfulness into my work routine and intentionally slowing down my pace in order to connect with my staff. I made it my priority to stop and have a cafe with co-workers, strike up casual conversations about food and family, and wander to other departments for no other reason other than to say ciao. I dedicated more time to having extended work lunches with wine (on me of course) and creating fun team-building activities where the team really got to know one another. Our interoffice camaraderie increased, and soon thereafter our collective work productivity noticeably increased. I am eternally grateful for the lessons I learned at the Italian job, and to this day I fondly recall and treasure the time I spent with those amazing people. They taught me the importance of human connection, relationships, and being truly present and engaged.

PART TWO: BACKGROUND

7 GROWING UP

"If you want to grow, know there will be growing pains." -Unknown

E ven after extensive reflection and deeper analysis on basic self-care, I felt like I was still missing several pieces to this complex puzzle. I could not shake the feeling that even if I had taken better care of my body and mind, this breakdown would have still happened. I decided to dig deeper, and I determined the best place to start was at the beginning of life itself.

I began by conducting extensive research on childhood development, directing my attention onto my own upbringing. What I learned was that while lack of self-care certainly contributed to my breakdown, it was definitely not the only contributing factor. As humans, our childhood years are critical developmental periods in our lives helping to shape our decision-making, personalities, emotional regulation and perspective on reality. In fact, this developmental period is crucial because a child's critical mind doesn't fully develop until around the age of eight. This means that everything a child experiences up to that point is stored in their subconscious without analysis, forcing them to perceive everything they experience as fact.

In fact, children are so sensitive to their environments that if a parent who is changing a child's diaper continually approaches this act with disgust, the child is far more likely to develop gastrointestinal issues later in life. Children absorb everything, so stop to think about all the things we tell children during this developmental stage: "Stop being such a baby!" "Why can't you do anything right?" "You aren't very smart, you will never amount to anything!" And perhaps the absolute worst one "I wish you were never born!" These expressions can be throwaway words to an adult but are absolute poison to a child, and they have long-term negative effects.

It was during this key developmental stage of childhood that I experienced a horrendous traumatic life-event, and at the age of seven I did not have the mental capacity to properly process what had happened. All I can remember is that afterward, I grew increasingly stressed out and anxious, and my head was flooded with worst case scenarios day and night. My brain believed that if I let my guard down something bad would happen to me again, so I had become perpetually vigilant. Over the years, the nagging, uncomfortable thoughts and emotions became more and more intense, and I discovered that when I ate my favorite foods these emotions would subside — at least temporarily. The problem was that I continued to eat and eat to cope, and eventually I gained an extra 20 pounds in my early teens. As we all know, kids at that age can be brutal and unforgiving: I was constantly teased and tormented because of my weight gain, and my mental health continued to decline even more.

After spending half of my freshman year depressed and friendless, often eating my lunch in a bathroom stall with tears running down my face, I thought I knew what I had to do. I had to change my external appearance, which would magically fix all my problems. My 13 year-old mind had it all figured out: if I could make my life appear perfect, then people would stop teasing me and start to treat me like an actual human being: So I began to work really hard — not at fixing my emotional state, but on totally reinventing my appearance and my level of popularity. I worked really hard to get good grades (check!), become captain of the swim team (check!), dated the captain of the football team (double check!), and lost an alarming amount of weight (triple check!). And here's the sad thing: people actually treated me differently, as if my appearance was the only thing about me that made me significant. My teachers suddenly behaved as if I was more intelligent, boys wanted to take me out on dates, and people started to treat me like I was finally worth something.

I was excellent at maintaining the illusion that everything in my life was perfect, but I was literally falling apart on the inside as my anxiety was progressively worsening. This continued for years.... and I then finally reached a crossroads. I was getting closer to graduating from high school, and I needed to make a decision about the next chapter in my life. The one thing I have always taken pride in was my kindheartedness: I have always had some innate sense that all humans are in some way suffering, and that it was my job to treat everyone I met with compassion. Moreover, I also felt a deeply personal drive to serve others, and this drive instilled in me big dreams of joining the Peace Corps.

Now, let me start off by saying that I love my parents and in no way do I think they did anything but their best for me. They come from humble, immigrant backgrounds where adversity and hardship were plentiful, and they believed that their main job as parents was for my brother and I to have a better life than they did. They also believed that there was a specific formula to success that had to be followed: you will play sports, you will get good grades, you will go to college, and then you will find a husband... and that unequivocally leads to life success. (And no, this formula was not up for debate.)

Most kids get kicked out of their house for doing drugs or skipping school; my parents threatened to kick me out because I had grandiose dreams of delaying college in order to join the Peace Corps. If you think I am exaggerating, I'm not: I was going to college and that was that, period and end of sentence. I reluctantly agreed, even though I had no idea where I would go to school, what I would study, or what I wanted to do as a career post-graduation. I simply and sadly agreed and I think this was the first time I consciously decided to play life's game out of a sense of obligation. I ignored what my heart wanted and immediately shifted to being more realistic, practical, and focusing on who I was supposed to become. I threw my dreams of working for the Peace Corps into the garbage and focused all of my energy on becoming the daughter my parents would be proud of, instead of a big fat failure that they would be embarrassed by. I was slowly starting to become more and more lost, and I was slowly morphing into the machine mindset where I needed to perform and be successful in order to please others.

What followed for the next decade was me making a series of life choices where I ignored my own needs and put everyone else in my life first. Every job I took, every relationship I was in, everything I did was out of a sense of obligation to make other people happy — I never once took a step back to ask myself why. And when something went wrong, or I was unhappy, I silently blamed others: "The relationship failed because of him." "I wasn't successful because my boss didn't support me." "I will never have a normal life." "I am broken." "The world is a horrible place that is against me." And the list went on and on. As I developed this victim mentality, I started to grow increasingly angry, resentful, and toxic. On top of that, my insomnia and anxiety worsened and I started to have paralyzing panic attacks, all culminating in that fateful day in Santorini.

I now understand that due to the traumatic event that occurred at age seven, my emotional regulation and several other key components for good mental health were stunted. I also lacked a strong sense of self, which made it difficult for me to understand and subsequently articulate my needs. This lack of development affected not only my thinking but my relationships with others.

The following chapters touch on some of the most important aspects of building healthy relationships with yourself and the people around you. It has taken me over 30 years to fully grasp some of these concepts, but, better late than never.

8 EMOTIONS

"You cannot control the behavior of others, but you can always choose how you respond to it." -Roy T. Bennett

E motions are not bad — in fact, they are a necessary part of life. They are a reflection of our past experiences and a gauge of our internal state. In this life, you will experience the highest of highs and the lowest of lows, and it is certainly not ideal to get in the habit of suppressing any of these emotions. The key is to find the correct balance between expressing emotions — in a healthy way, and for a reasonable amount of time — and then making the conscious decision to move past negative ones. What is reasonable? Well, the definition is up to you. Innately, you will know when it's time to move on, and you just need to learn to trust your intuition.

Pain, grief, sadness and anger are normal emotions, and they should be expressed. Just bear in mind that the more you focus your attention on a negative experience or emotion, the more you strengthen that neural circuit in your brain. An example that I think we can all relate to is road rage. We have all been in the situation where someone on their cell phone isn't paying attention, then unexpectedly changes lanes and forces you to swerve off the highway. When this happens, what is your reaction? Do you take a deep breath, look around and make sure you are okay, and then continue your drive to work? Or do you roll down your window, give that person a piece of your mind, continue that rant the entire way to work, and then proceed to share that story with every one of your co-workers?

You have to really ask yourself: is it worth it to spend your limited energy on a stranger who you will literally never ever see again in your entire life? I know it is difficult, but think of the plethora of other things that you could have spent your time, focus, and attention on. As painful as it might be, I always try my best to not engage when emotional situations arise. I don't always succeed, but I do try. I believe that great power lies in the ability to exhibit self-control and not react emotionally to these situations... but ultimately the choice is yours.

Another important point to keep in mind is that the specific brain networks responsible for conscious decision making shut down when you are emotional. For this reason, it is crucial to not make rash decisions or react when you are in an elevated emotional state. How many of us have written an email or text that we later regretted? I definitely have. When emotional situations arise — as they always do — try your best to remove yourself from the situation. And please don't return until your emotional circuits are no longer firing and you can tap into the rational decision making centers of your brain and react in a way that you won't regret. I promise you will thank me later.

Learning to effectively manage your emotions is one of the most powerful and important skills to master in your lifetime. This does not mean you should put your needs on the back burner or bury them down deep until you are like a volcano about to explode. What it means is that you need to be in touch with your current state of mind every day, and throughout every hour of every day. You need to constantly ask yourself if you are hungry, if you need a nap, if you feel happy or sad, etc. I know this might sound silly, but the majority of us keep pushing forward throughout the day without stopping to see how we feel or what we need. Then we end up burning out or having a meltdown.

"Respond versus react" is a mantra I repeat to myself when I encounter a challenging person or situation, and this normally helps to provide me with perspective. However, in order to attain the mental state where you can be adequately and properly responsive, it is important to work on incorporating mindfulness (which we have already touched on) and boundaries (more on these to come) into your life. These two tools are crucial in keeping one's emotions in check so that when an emotional situation does arise you are able to engage from a place of control, grace and poise. I assure you that over time and with practice, you will notice that your emotional triggers will start to weaken and you won't become as frustrated when answering a provocative email or communicating with a challenging individual. And if you happen to slip up and let your emotions get the best of you, don't beat yourself up. We are all human.... and you will always have more opportunities to try again and get better.

9 RELATIONSHIPS

"A healthy relationship doesn't drag you down, it inspires you to be better." -Mandy Hale

Once you have your internal state and emotions in balance, it's time to start tackling your interpersonal relationships. There are several components to emotional intelligence and healthy relationships: open communication, boundaries, and honesty. It is fundamental to first understand your needs and values, and then find a way to calmly and clearly communicate your needs with those around you. You are not a mindreader, therefore you cannot expect those around you to be able to read your mind. Life would also be a lot easier if you can be up front and honest about who you are, and give others the freedom to do the same without judgement.

Before diving into your interactions with others, let's begin with your most important relationship of all: you. I have the best company in the world at my disposal 24-7, which is myself. Regardless of what you have been spoon-fed, it is completely OK to be alone. In fact, it is important to be able to be alone with all your thoughts, insecurities, and fears without the crutch of a cell phone, social media, television, alcohol, or drugs to distract you from the process of self-deconstruction and self-analysis that eventually leads to self-improvement.

And though it sounds cliche, you will never be capable of fully loving someone else unless and until you learn to love yourself. There is no point in trying to have a serious, meaningful relationship with someone until you come to a place of peace with yourself where you accept yourself exactly as you are, in this very moment, without trying to change a thing.

Friendships

"The principal difference between heaven and hell is the company you keep there." -Lois McMaster Bujold

At the point of my breakdown I felt isolated, alone, and over-whelmed. Living in another country where I could only speak the language on a superficial level made creating and maintaining meaningful relationships extremely difficult. I had a few American friends, but for the most part I lacked a strong support network in my life. I felt like an outsider who didn't belong and was hesitant to trust due to all the past pain and ridicule I had endured, and to make things worse I absolutely hated asking people for help. At the time I thought it was a sign of weakness, and I also loathed the thought of being a burden to others. However, none of this was actually true, and if I had taken the time and energy to build a stronger support network, it would have made this period of my life more manageable.

Indeed, there is solid science to back up my claim. In the Wall Street Journal article *The Surprising Science Behind Friendship*, researchers examined friendship's effect on physical health and determined it has positive benefits on cardiovascular function, immune strength, and even sleep.[18] Additionally, a study conducted among Harvard men ages 20 to 80 found that the single most important predictor of health and happiness at 80 had nothing to do with professional success or money and everything to do with, quality of their relationships.[19] This result begs the question: What defines a good friendship? According to this same Harvard study, biologists define a friendship as positive if "it makes you feel good, it is long-lasting and stable, and has reciprocity and co-operation in it."[19]

Other than the ones with yourself and your family, the most important relationships you possess are your friendships. While you cannot choose your family, you can most certainly choose your friends. We all come to a point in our lives where we must take a step back and evaluate the company we keep. If you haven't done so just yet, you might want to ask yourself the following questions: Do you feel happy, inspired, and encouraged when you spend time with a specific person? Or do you feel tired, negative and defeated? At the end of the day, the people you surround yourself with are either providing you with energy, or else draining energy from you.

In addition to the emotional state you experience around people, you also need to be cognizant of the quality of your engagement with individuals. One of my favorite philosophers was Socrates, who taught his students that "strong minds discuss ideas, average minds discuss events, and weak minds discuss people." This is a powerful statement because as you begin to examine conversations you have, you start to notice that you have friends who do nothing but complain and gossip. Then on the opposite end of the spectrum, you have friends that are happy, encouraging, and excited to talk about how they are living their best lives, and they encourage and support you to do the same. It should make no difference whether you have known a person for months or since you were five years old, you have no obligation to give your time and attention to them if they are toxic. You need to start focusing on yourself, your time, your energy and the person you wish to become.

Healthy friendships are crucial to your well-being because you cannot depend on one person — best friend, spouse, sibling — to fulfill all of your needs. We all need a network of people in our lives to celebrate life's joyous occasions and to hold our hand through life's inevitable hardships. Relationships should be a give-and-take partnership, and you should work to continually nurture these connections. Don't worry if you have less friends as you get older, just make sure they are quality people. Here is my litmus test for a good friend:

1. If a loved one died, would this person call immediately and tell you that they would get on the first flight from halfway around the world to help?
2. Would they be willing to bail you out of jail, without judgement, with their first words being "are you OK"?
3. Can you pick up the phone after not speaking for a year and call them out of the blue, and the conversation between you two not skip a beat?

Reflecting back on my life, I definitely have had some friendships that I held onto far too long out of a sense of obligation, but that's OK. I approached these people to express my concerns about our relationships as openly and honestly as I could, and when I never heard back I knew it was time to move on. I also recognized that some friends were drinking buddies, and the relationship was simply never going to mature beyond drinking buddies — and that's perfectly fine, too.

On the opposite end of the spectrum, I do have some really awesome friends that would pass the three litmus tests above: Colleen, Maribeth, Kim, Molly, and Rossman. These were my Gamma Phi Beta sorority sisters who I met over twenty years ago during my undergraduate studies at Penn State. As I write this today, we still have an active group chat where we keep in touch and discuss important issues like what we wore to fraternity socials in the late 90s and who was hotter, Pacey or Dawson? (Pacey of course.)

In this circle of friends, we have dealt with numerous weighty topics — marriages, divorces, babies, cancer and even death. I can say without hesitation that there are no other people in this world I wanted by my side during such challenging life events. I would not be the resilient woman I am today if I did not have their love, encouragement and support, and because of that I remain deeply committed to continuing to cultivate these relationships for the rest of my life.

Reflecting once more on my past work relationships in Italy, I learned a very powerful lesson: nobody in this world is a burden, and there are many people including myself who receive great joy in helping others. So whether you need someone to review a term paper for school, a helping hand when you are stuck in bed with the flu, or a shoulder to cry on when things just couldn't get any worse, I hope you do not hesitate to ask such friends for their help. Never think of yourself as being a burden, and don't deny friends like myself who harbor that giving mindset the joy of helping you. Helping friends also makes the helper feel supported — I for one know that such friends will be there for me when I inevitably fall once more and need someone to pick me back up.

I'd like for my readers to challenge themselves by reflecting on both their relationships with self and their relationships with close friends. Are the majority of these interactions meaningful and positive, or are they laborious and leave you feeling heavy, exhausted, and negative? If there is a relationship that is not adding value to your life, do you feel like you could approach the other party from a place of love and openly express your feelings, or is it simply time to stop putting in effort? As for the meaningful and positive relationships, I would suggest reaching out to someone you have not spoken to in awhile and just let them know you were thinking about them. We truly never know how much time we have, so why not spend this time showing the people you value that you genuinely care about them?

Dating

"A relationship is only as strong as the two people in it." -Chelsea Leigh Trescott

I can honestly say that until I had my breakdown, I took a very casual approach to dating and I didn't foresee that it could take such a considerable toll on my mental and physical health. I decided to explore in more depth the science of dating, and I learned that people involved in loving relationships have healthier immune systems, make fewer doctor visits and shorter hospital stays, experience less physical pain, and live longer.[20] Emotional benefits include increased resilience, lower rates of anxiety and depression, higher self-esteem, greater empathy, and an improved quality of life.[21] Conversely, the tension caused by the intense conflict in an unhealthy or abusive relationship can keep one's body in fight-or-flight mode, continually forcing your body to produce excess adrenaline. Over time, this pressure will result in fatigue, weakened immune system, and even organ damage.[22]

Armed with the knowledge that choosing a partner will have some effect on your physical and mental well-being, you might want to slow down and take some time to reflect before jumping into that next relationship. Before your next date, take some time to contemplate your life goals and what you want out of a relationship, and don't be afraid to dig deep. Dating because you are sad, lonely or bored is probably one of the worst things that you can do for your emotional stability. Look, I get it: every person will experience some degree of sadness, loneliness, and emptiness in their life, and those emotions are very uncomfortable. Some people choose to escape this discomfort by binge watching TV; others drink excessively, or abuse food, sex, or drugs. But you need to understand that when you date just because you are sad, lonely or bored, you are likely ignoring some underlying and more pressing emotional need. It won't be easy, but it would certainly be more beneficial for your long-term health to explore and unpack that discomfort on your own — then strategize healthy ways to alleviate it — versus filling the void with distracting or unhealthy solutions.

This leads directly into my next question: why are so many people in unhealthy relationships? I, for one, have to place some of the blame on entertainment. Everywhere on TV and in the movies, we are inundated with unrealistic love stories and rom-coms that have no basis in reality. Naturally, we compare our lives to these stories and become disappointed when our relationships don't reflect what we see. This is also true with music — most popular songs are about how the artist can't live without someone, the pain of someone leaving him or her, or the sadness he or she feels for being alone. This is arguably the worst message we can be sending in regards to healthy relationships. You do not need someone to complete you; rather, you need to put in the individual work to be happy, healthy, and whole on your own before you even think about entering into a serious relationship. It is not someone else's job to fix or save you, nor should that ever be required of you.

However, this is also easier said than done, particularly since the entire paradigm of dating has shifted over the past few decades. When I first started dating many moons ago, the world was a totally different place. You had to call someone — not on their smartphone, but on their home phone landline — to coordinate a time and date. Your date would pick you up at your home and it was expected that he or she would deliver you back there safely at the end of the night. Great time and effort would be spent on planning these dates, and your date nearly always refused to allow you to pay, even if you insisted. Oh, those were the good old days.

Today's dating world is full of apps, emojis, texts, instant gratification, label-less relationships, ghosting, flaky behavior and an endless number of options. And that's just the tip of the iceberg: these apps teach us that people are disposable, take the work out of building long-term relationships, make cheating more convenient and less likely to be caught, and allow people to lie about themselves. Recent research suggests that dating apps also negatively impact self-esteem and that the more time you spend looking for love online, the more likely you are to experience depression and anxiety.[23] One study published by the American Psychological Association reveals that, "...being actively involved with Tinder, regardless of the user's gender, was associated with body dissatisfaction, body shame, body monitoring, internalization of societal expectations of beauty, comparing oneself physically to others, and reliance on media for information on appearance and attractiveness."[24]

On the other side of the spectrum, I know that there are some people who have had great success with online dating apps, and as evidence I recently attended a wedding where the couple met online. So if you do decide to go that route, experts recommend approaching online dating from a healthy headspace. They also suggest being honest, putting a limit on your daily use, reaching out with positivity and kindness, and establishing good boundaries so as to decrease the chances of ghosting or a toxic chat.[25] Another expert recommendation is to try to maintain a positive attitude when the date does not go as planned, and instead of sulking and complaining that you will be forever single, shift your point of view to the much more positive mindset that you are wiser and one step closer to finding your true partner.

Instead of participating in online dating, I work to live my best life through numerous hobbies, travels, studies, and making a conscious effort to engage organically with as many people as possible along the way. I also live with the confidence that everything will happen exactly when it is supposed to and without me forcing it. Yes, there are plenty of occasions when I feel lonely — holidays, vacations, and the worst of all, Valentine's Day — but I find comfort in the fact that the grass is always greener and that not everything about being in a relationship is all sunshine and roses. For example, I can do whatever the hell I want, whenever I want. I can pack up a suitcase and move halfway across the world and not have to ask permission from anyone (well, except my cat). As much as I would love to be in a mutual partnership, I find solace in the independence I now have and take advantage of that freedom to live my daily life more fully.

When it comes to dating, here is my final advice: know your self-worth, have confidence in your own inner strength, and be genuinely grateful for the relationships that don't work out. Everyone comes into your life to teach you something about yourself and/or the world around you. Discover those lessons, learn to let people go, and let them go with love — no matter how much it might hurt. Then, learn not to repeat the mistakes of your past in your future relationships. Eventually, you will meet someone that you do not need, but love to be around regardless. Someone who loves you exactly as you are, with all your awesomeness and all your flaws. Someone who inspires you to be the best version of yourself without saying a word, and whose future goals are in alignment with yours. Someone who is there to pick you up when you inevitably fall and is proud to have you by their side.

In the meantime, be patient and have faith that everything you desire will happen at exactly the right time, exactly as it should. And most importantly, please remember that it is always better to be alone than to be in bad company, and that you should never have to decrease your awesomeness to make other people more comfortable.

10 BOUNDARIES & DETACHMENT

"Sometimes you have to teach people how to treat you." -Oprah Winfrey

Boundaries — ahh, what a concept. This was a word I did not learn, or at least I did not fully understand its true meaning, until I was in my mid-30s. Boundaries are rules and guidelines that you create to show others how to treat you. They help to establish clear expectations and needs in your relationships, and are based on your own core beliefs. Boundaries are a measure of self-esteem and they help to ensure that relationships are mutually respectful. Creating healthy boundaries is important because they help us to be more compassionate to others' needs while ensuring that our own are still met.

Research shows there is a clear psychological cost of never saying no: unhealthy relationships, resentment, stress, anxiety, depression, burnout, and lack of personal identity.[26] Some people have difficulty setting boundaries because they were taught that it was rude to do so, or they are afraid to establish them on account of past trauma or abuse. Others struggle to set boundaries due to fear of missing out, perfectionism, or social conditioning.[27] Whatever the source of the cause, the effects are clear: if you don't set boundaries, then you will likely find yourself at the mercy of others tending towards valuing other people more than yourself, which can lead to feelings of being lost and frustrated.

For me, it was all of the above during that period when I lacked any sense of boundaries in my life. I agreed to every social invitation, work assignment, and personal favor that was asked of me. I allowed bosses and coworkers to speak to me in a demeaning manner and assumed that this was just normal behavior. I made excuses for past boyfriends when they behaved poorly by taking advantage of my kindness or being cruel to me. I told myself that they were stressed, they didn't mean it, they simply needed my love and patience. I actually believed that I was obligated to bend over backwards and ensure that everyone in my life was taken care of and that it was my responsibility to be the glue to fix every situation, and if I did so then everyone would be happy. But in reality, the people taking advantage of me and my lack of boundaries realized they could simply abuse me more and it eventually took its toll on me.

That was until I met Monica.

Several years ago I was surfing online when an ad for a self-help course entitled *Learn How to Build A More Confident You* — produced by inspirational lifestyle brand mindbodygreen — popped up on my screen. I was intrigued: At this exact point in my life, I felt I could definitely use more confidence. I proceeded to click on the ad and was greeted by an image of a beautiful woman with olive skin, dark hair, and a smile that could light up a room. That woman was Monica Parikh, the founder and CEO of School of Love NYC, and that online course was the beginning of a relationship that I deeply treasure and intend to keep for years to come.

I immediately signed up for and began the first course; Monica's intuition, insight, and advice was so on point that I immediately thirsted for more. Once I graduated from her online course, I signed up for both her group sessions and individual coaching. In one of my first classes with Monica, she spent an entire hour discussing the act of giving. She explained that you can only give when you have liquid in the saucer. This means that if your cup is half-empty, you should focus on filling it back up. However, when your cup is overflowing into the saucer, then you can decide IF you want to give. This is how you avoid the overgiving that leads to burnout. Again, you need to be in touch with your emotions and self-needs in order to properly identify when it is time to give and when it is time to receive and rest, and this is a powerful lesson to those of us that have been plagued by too much giving.

Monica has also taught me a great deal about boundaries, how to establish them, how to communicate them, and most importantly what to do when they are violated. She stresses that boundaries must have actionable consequences that you stand by, and these rules should not change whether you are dealing with a lover, co-worker or even your own mother (sorry Mom). You are the most important person in this world and you are not, and never have been, obligated to do anything. (I want you to stop, pause, and read that sentence aloud again.) Regardless of what has been ingrained in your head since childhood, feelings of obligation and guilt are just that: they are feelings, not facts. And as soon as you can establish that they are not facts, the sooner your life will begin to dramatically change for the better.

Monica's courses and mindset taught me that I need to establish healthy boundaries with all of the people in my life and that it's also important to detach myself from any particular outcomes. This means consistently striving to communicate clearly and calmly what I need from others, being able to say no when I want to, and being able to accept when someone tells me no (hence the detachment). And on the occasion that someone is not willing to respect my boundaries, then it is my responsibility to walk away gracefully.

I want to encourage you to evaluate your relationships and ask yourself if you have healthy boundaries. Do you have non-negotiable boundaries in your romantic and professional relationships, what are the consequences, and how do you work to enforce them? How do you respond when a family member has violated a boundary? Do you understand that some people are just broken and it is not your job to fix them? I know first-hand how much hard work and mental discipline it takes to begin setting boundaries, but I promise you that once you start getting into the habit of doing so it gets easier and easier to keep them and benefit from them. And if you are worried about hurting someone's feelings, then just try to remember that you are putting the most important person in the world — YOU — first and foremost.

11 BLAME, RESPONSIBILITY & THE PAST

"When you blame others, you give up your power to change." -Robert Anthony

As I reflected more and more on this tumultuous period of my life, one of the most difficult lessons for me to learn was responsibility. Surely you have noticed that I reiterate this theme several times throughout this book. This is intentional because acceptance of what is — and taking responsibility for your role in it — is a critical and non-negotiable component of self-growth. I spent the majority of my life blaming EVERYONE. I blamed my weight fluctuations on having bad genes; I blamed my anxiety on enduring a terrible childhood; the world was a cruel place, and it was my parents' fault, or my brother's, or my boss's, or my boyfriend's. I was the victim, and I had no control of or agency to my circumstances.

I gradually matured and came to the realization that I needed to shift from these unhealthy thought patterns. I started researching the science of blame, otherwise known in the field of psychology as blame shifting. Blame shifting is defined as an emotionally abusive behavior or tactic where abusers struggle with taking responsibility for their life choices and problems, and they refuse to accept ownership of their emotions.[28] Blame shifting is detrimental because it interferes with our ability to experience self-worth, enhances our feelings of victimhood, and it diminishes our ability to develop resilience.[29]

After studying the psychology of blame, I shifted my focus to understanding how the brain processes and stores past experiences. I learned that when an event occurs, our brains automatically store this experience in our short-term memory. Depending on the importance of the event and the level of emotion it has evoked, the brain may induce protein synthesis and convert this to long-term memory — this process is known as memory consolidation. Then your brain stores memories similar to how Blockbuster® managed their DVDs: Every time you recall the memory, it is akin to taking a DVD off the shelf and watching it on a home theater, then later returning the DVD to its original owner (for our younger crowd, you may want to ask your parents about the days when movies were consumed through DVD rentals instead of internet streaming). Every time you replay the scene in your mind, your brain undergoes another phase of protein synthesis, and then you place that event back into storage. This is the process of memory reconsolidation, which serves to maintain, strengthen and modify long-term memories.[30]

However, you have to keep in mind (pun intended) that every time you recall a memory, you change aspects of the event; furthermore, if you block protein synthesis, you block memory storage. The positive benefits of this phenomenon are that you can ingrain new information into old memories, and you can also dampen the emotional component of negative or traumatic events.[31] The negative aspects are that you change details of past events in your mind, which can cloud your ability to describe what actually happened. While researchers continue to debate exact percentages, they calculate that somewhere between 40-60% of memories are in some way altered, if not flat-out false.

Emotion also plays a crucial role in memory formation: strongly charged memories are hard-wired more intensely in our brains. It is for this reason that you can tell me exactly where you were when you received the tragic news about the events of 9-11, but you will have trouble telling me what you had for dinner last Tuesday.

Now then, let's use this science for your benefit. Suppose I have just been set up on a blind date with the man of my dreams. It was love at first sight and we dated for months. He was funny and charismatic, met my parents, and spoke earnestly about marriage and babies. Then one day out of nowhere, poof! — he disappears without a trace. After a few weeks of heartbreak followed by a few weeks of speculative overthinking, I am fairly confident he went back to the wife and kids that he had temporarily deserted because he was having a midlife crisis. For me, this is going to be an emotionally devastating event — I was planning our future and picking out our children's names, and now he's gone without any explanation or apology.

In this hypothetical scenario, I am now at a crossroads where I need to make a serious decision. On one hand, I can stew in my vengeance-fueled anger, stalk his social media, find his wife and family and spend the next year crafting the perfect plan to ruin this man's life. OR, I can capitalize on this knowledge of how my brain stores memories and work to move forward by engaging in a process I call "Write Any Story You Want." As discussed above, neuroscientific studies have proven that you can add new information to memories during the memory reconsolidation phase, but what's even more interesting is that the more detailed, outrageous, and comical the details you add to the story, the more you can dampen the emotional impact of the memory.[32]

Back to our scenario: after a few days of getting over the initial shock and quelling my emotions so I can make rational decisions, I sit down at my computer and craft a story. This man was actually a Russian spy who was in the U.S. to get intel on when dinosaurs would be outfitted with laser beams and he thought I was a top-secret paleontologist. Stupid story? Yes. But over time, the story grows increasingly effective because every time I start to feel sadness or anger about this situation I return to this ridiculous story and add more colorful details. Then each time I am reminded of the hurt, I will experience slightly less pain and emotional reactions than the time before, until I get to the point where I can finally just let it go completely and move on.

This technique can also be used for non-traumatic thoughts and memories — for example, when you apply to a coveted job, follow up with the human resource manager daily for a month, and receive no response or a rejection. Or when you text your best friend but she doesn't reply for the next 24 hours, so you begin to go through all the worst case scenarios where you might have offended or upset her. Instead of worrying, try crafting an outlandish story and let it go, because in most cases the second we remove our energy from this one situation we finally receive an answer, and it is 99.999% of the time NOT the worst case scenario that we concocted in our head.

We all have memories that we want to forget. I can think of dozens of life moments where I longed to be the character Jim Carrey plays in the movie *Eternal Sunshine of the Spotless Mind* so that I could have people and events erased permanently from my brain. Until that technology is fully developed — or until time machines are perfected, whichever comes first — give the "Write Any Story You Want" technique a try. Then continue to ask yourself: "When (not if, but when) should I let go?" Specifically, you are not letting go of the memory — but you need to let go of the anger, the rage, the resentment.

I believe that forgiveness is an act not an emotion, and a memory without emotion is wisdom. (You might want to pause once more, reread that sentence, and let that one really soak in.) Waiting for someone to apologize or agonizing over past hurt merely wastes your own energy. So accept what is and find a way to move on, no matter how painful it may be right now. Every single day you have a choice: you can wake up and choose to be a victim, or you can choose to be an agent creator of your life. You can blame others for your life's circumstances, or you can take responsibility for your past choices and make better choices today to create your ideal future. What choice will you make today?

PART THREE: BREAKTHROUGH

12 MOVING TO A HIGHER FREQUENCY

"If you are going through hell, keep going." -Winston Churchill

Meanwhile, back in Greece...

Due to my mental breakdown while in Santorini, I cut my idyllic vacation short and returned home to Italy feeling exhausted, deflated and utterly confused. I knew my life had to change, so from that point on I made a firm decision with willful intention: I was going to be the creator of my life and not the victim. I literally wiped my brain clean of every fact, goal, value, rule and tenet that I had been taught and embarked on a journey to discover my truth. I knew it was not going to be easy, that I was likely going to piss off a lot of people, and to be honest I did not yet have a gameplan. However, one thing I was confident about was that I could not keep living like this. I decided to become the scientist of my own life, and thus I began an experimental journey filled with exotic travel, unique people and valuable lessons learned. This is where my story gets a lot more interesting and a lot more fun... and oh, a lot more weird.

13 THERAPY

"You are not broke, you are breaking through." -Alex Myles

When I returned from what should have been one of the most romantic trips of my life, my mind was in a chaotic state. I wasn't quite sure where to begin, but I figured reaching out to a professional would be a good start. I had not worked with a coach or therapist in the past but I was desperate for some direction, so I reached out to Louise Smart, an energy consultant in London. The founder of Emotional Detox, Louise specializes in stress management, energy clearing and emotional detoxification. I was intrigued by her unconventional background and training, and figured "What the hell, let's give it a shot!" After all, in my mind at the time I felt like I could not get any worse.

When I first contacted Louise, I had no expectations of what our sessions would look like or if she could actually help me, but I kept an open mind. I can still clearly remember the first time we connected: she had this radiant calm that I could actually sense over the phone, and she made me feel at ease. My mind was racing a million miles a minute, but when she spoke I felt my thoughts slow down dramatically. While the initial sense of calm that she provided me didn't last long it was definitely a good start.

We spoke for about an hour and I shared with her my struggles, anxiety, panic attacks, sleeplessness and depression. She listened calmly and intently, and never once stopped to interrupt. When I was finished with my laundry list of ailments, she paused and asked me to close my eyes and take a deep breath. Then she asked me to try again, to speak more slowly and to fill up my abdomen and breathe in for five seconds and then breathe out at the same pace. And as silly as it may sound, I could not complete this simple request. She said it sounded like I was taking short, shallow breaths which could be contributing to my anxiety and panic attacks, and she was right.

What I now realize is that when I entered a new situation or was nervous, I stopped breathing properly which in turn sent a feedback signal to my body that I was in danger. This would result in shallow breathing, dizziness, lightheadedness and confusion. I physically felt like I was dying, which was not far from the truth since in these moments my body would stop breathing. Over time and with practice, I have become more aware of when this respiratory arrest occurs, and I remind myself to pause and take a long, slow breath. This simple yet highly effective advice has become an invaluable tool that has greatly reduced my anxiety and propensity for panic attacks.

After several weeks of working with me, Louise also recognized that I had this overwhelming feeling of being uncomfortable in my own skin. I used to describe my body as this tired, heavy lump of mass that obstinately resisted my every movement, and every time I tried to accomplish a task it would make doing so as difficult as possible. Louise asked me to try incorporating a few simple activities in my weekly routine. She wanted me to substitute my triple espresso coffees with herbal tea, alternate yoga for high-intensity weight training classes, and find time to get a weekly massage. She also sent me several sleep hypnosis audio tracks to help me relax my body and fall asleep more quickly.

None of this was groundbreaking or that difficult to follow, so I agreed. After about a month of heeding her advice, I started sleeping again — well, only two hours a night but that was a noticeable improvement from zero. Clearly it was going to take awhile to unlearn all the bad habits and negative thinking patterns that had been wired into my brain and conditioned into my body for the past three decades, but it was a start.

At first I was confused about Louise's prescription for my ailments, but I now understand that she was using basic techniques to calm my nervous system, which had been in overdrive for years. The nervous system, which is your body's electrical wiring system, is divided into the autonomic nervous system (think automatic or involuntary) and the somatic nervous system (which is voluntary). The somatic nervous system controls movement via skeletal muscles, while the autonomic nervous system works without any conscious effort to control processes like digestion, metabolism, body temperature, heartbeat and breathing rate. The autonomic nervous system can be further subdivided into the sympathetic nervous system (SNS) and the parasympathetic nervous system (PNS). The responsibility of the PNS is to keep the body from overloading and thus it works to preserve a calm and balanced metabolic state. Conversely, the SNS prepares the body for the fight-or-flight response and shifts energy resources toward addressing and fighting a threat in one's immediate environment.

In my case, my body was so stressed that my SNS was continuously stimulated and signaling my body to release cortisol, the stress hormone, and increase my blood sugar levels, which in turn stressed my heart and my immune system. On a cognitive level, I was not capable of thinking clearly because my amygdala, the region of the brain where we assign meaning to emotions, was classifying all incoming information as threatening.[33] This would explain why I could not make calm, rational decisions and why I was always on guard and expecting the worst case scenario.

Our bodies are designed to handle stress in small doses and even benefit from these controlled amounts, but when stress is chronic it becomes detrimental. So when should you be concerned that stress might be taking its toll on your body? I would suggest taking an assessment of your current health. Do you have frequent tension-type headaches or migraines? Do you suffer from shortness of breath, rapid breathing, or stress-induced asthma attacks? Side note: your gut is inhabited by millions of bacteria that influence your body organs and brain, and chronic stress can result in GI disease and discomfort, bloating gut pain or other dysfunction. If you suffer from prolonged heartburn, acid reflux, nausea and/or vomiting then please reach out to your healthcare professional, who will be able to help you to identify individual challenges and stressors and design treatments to mitigate your pain and discomfort.

Louise was an excellent resource for me to begin my healing journey. She was able to view my problems from a different perspective and provide reasonable, realistic solutions. I understand that it might be uncomfortable to share your deepest fears and anxieties with a stranger, however in practice many do find it easier to share their problems with someone they don't know — someone highly trained and certified who can offer clinical solutions without emotion, judgment or resentment. I highly recommend professional coaches and therapists because we all need a team of qualified people to support us through different transition stages in our lives. And much like I discussed in the previous relationships chapter, it is unrealistic to depend on one person (spouse, sibling, friend, etc.) to be your rock, to support you and give you advice all the time.

If you think you could benefit from a therapist or coach, it's best to begin by understanding the difference between the two classifications, and then decide which of each best fits your needs. A therapist is a healthcare professional who is licensed to treat long-term emotional issues and trauma; a coach helps you to solve complex problems and achieve your goals by providing motivation, support, resources and roadmaps. If you are looking to clarify and achieve personal and professional goals, work-life balance, or improve your cognitive or emotional health, then a coach might be a good option for you. On the other hand, if you want to explore a traumatic event, destructive relationship, or work through depression or anxiety that affects your ability to function at work or home, you might want to contact a therapist or other healthcare professional.

I also want to caution you that if you are going to invest time and money into one of these professionals, that you need to do your research and find one who is both knowledgeable and that you feel comfortable working with. I am speaking from experience because I have had some exceptional coaches and therapists, and I have also invested in others where I felt deflated and confused after speaking with them. I once hired a spiritual coach who sent me videos of her dancing around in a tube top. Needless to say, that relationship did not work out and I ended up losing several hundred dollars. This is why I strongly recommend a trial period or free introductory session where you can see if you and your coach are on the same page, work well together and are a good fit. And even though I am a coach myself, I still reach out to my network of coaches and therapists when I encounter a situation where I need guidance, support or an unbiased perspective.

14 SENSORY DEPRIVATION CHAMBERS

"Your imagination should be used not to escape reality but to create it." -Colin Wilson

After working with Louise for nearly a year, I came to the realization that I needed to find healthier ways to relax and calm my nervous system. I was straining to undo three decades of damage to my body as quickly as possible, and while months of therapy had been helpful, I wasn't going to be fully cured so soon. I began listening to podcasts and reading everything I could get my hands on in terms of self-care and mental health, and I stumbled upon a sensory deprivation chambers podcast from Joe Rogan, a wildly popular podcast host and sports announcer who most people also recognize as the host of the well-known network game show Fear Factor. Rogan spoke of the sensory deprivation chamber as the most important tool he ever used for developing his mind and evolving. He described his physical experience as light and vibrant, and explained that he used the chamber to contemplate and resolve major issues in his life. I was mesmerized by the description of his experience and assumed this was the key to my peace. All I needed was to find one of these chambers and all of my problems would be magically solved, right?

I started this journey with some research and discovered that the first chamber was designed in 1954 by John C. Lilly, an American physician, psychologist, and neuroscientist. Lilly was researching human consciousness, and he wanted to explore what would happen if he eliminated all sensory inputs to the brain. To test his hypothesis, he created a sensory deprivation chamber filled with hundreds of pounds of saltwater that he heated to the same temperature as resting body temperature with all external stimulation, including sight, sound, and gravity removed.[34]

What Lilly found was that these tanks helped his test subjects to achieve a state of deep relaxation while simultaneously producing a significant increase in theta-brainwave activity. At that time, this result was a scientific marvel because theta brainwaves, which were typically only observed during deep sleep, mediation, and hypnosis, had powerful mind-body healing qualities. This powerful brainwave state can be induced by certain mental exercises and have been shown to lower stress and anxiety as well as facilitate physical healing and growth. It is also the brainwave state that provides humans with access to our subconscious minds, boosts our immune system, and increases the faculties of intuition, creativity, learning, long-term memory, and emotional connection to feelings.

Physiologically speaking, the tank is filled with magnesium sulfate (i.e., Epsom salt) which is excellent for combating stress, alleviating muscular aches and pain, and reaching a relaxed state. Soaking in these salts has also been shown to stimulate lymph drainage and promote absorption of magnesium and sulphates. If you recall from the earlier chapter on sleep I mentioned the calming effects of magnesium. More than just promoting a state of relaxation, magnesium also helps to regulate the activity of more than 300 enzymes and performs a vital role in bodily functions such as muscle control and toxin elimination.[35] Research also suggests that elevating your magnesium and sulphate levels may relieve pain, improve heart and circulatory health and nerve function via electrolyte regulation, and aid in the prevention of migraine headaches.

Quite interestingly, across numerous research sources that I evaluated the words "sensory deprivation chambers" and "enlightenment" were used interchangeably to the point of being synonymous. Search engines returned web pages and articles titled *A Literal Shortcut to Enlightenment, Float to Enlightenment,* and *Science Can Help You Reach Enlightenment.* Thus, these chambers sounded like the perfect and convenient solution to all my problems.

I found my first tank in Berlin, but upon arrival I realized the translation into English was not correct because this ended up being a float spa and not a sensory deprivation chamber. These float tanks are essentially mini-relaxation spas, and although they were rare back in 2014 they can now be found in most major cities. The experience in Berlin was nice and relaxing, but I did not have the existential experience I so badly desired, so I decided to try again.

I began another search and found a chamber in Bergamo, Italy which is just outside Milan. Bergamo is a lovely walled-in city with an enchanting medieval atmosphere that looks like something out of a romantic Italian film. I reached out to the owner of the chamber and requested three, one-hour sessions on three consecutive days. In my mind I was a churning computational machine determined to discover the answer to all my problems, and this latest scheme had to be it. I went in with the expectation that I was going to head home feeling amazing and in possession of all of the answers to life's great questions.

What actually happened was the complete opposite. The first time I entered the chamber, it felt like I was laying in a wet coffin, and when they closed the heavy metal door into blackness, it felt like I was being buried alive. There is no light, no sound, no sense of touch — nothing. The basic concept of a sensory deprivation chamber is that it deprives you of all your senses so you have to focus internally. I assumed this internal reflection would be the key to my enlightenment, but I could not have been more wrong. Given my anxiety-ridden state at the time, I had not yet developed the capacity nor the mechanisms to shut down my inner voice and mindfully reflect inward. So instead of a state of relaxation, my mind shifted into hyperactive overdrive. Every fear, anxiety, worry, and worst-case scenario popped into my head within a matter of seconds of lying down in that tank. The first one-hour session was an absolute nightmare. I left that day feeling pissed off, defeated, and wondering why I couldn't have the magical experience that Joe Rogan had and that the Bergamo company's website touted.

On day two I woke up from a night of restless snoozing, dusted off my physical ailments and emotional wounds from the prior session, and went back into that chamber ready to fight. I laid down and took a deep breath... and then the next hour again felt like a miserable eternity. By day three, I was defeated — I spent just 15 minutes in the tank and then decided to get myself out. This method clearly was not working for me, and even worse I was making myself sicker by trying to force it.

In light of my dark experience (pun intended), I would suggest that you approach sensory deprivation chambers with caution. If you are an experienced meditator who is looking to reflect inward and my description of the wet coffin does not rattle you, then go for it. However, if you are high-anxiety and/or claustrophobic these chambers are probably not the best option, as your mind can spin out of control and you may end up with anxiety and fear rather than relaxation.

As for float spas, I highly recommend them for treating stress and enhancing creativity, performance, and insightful thought, not to mention for the plethora of other health benefits I listed above. I work to incorporate at least one visit per month and find that I always leave feeling energized, refreshed and renewed.

15

NEUROFEEDBACK RETREAT

"You can't solve a problem from the same level of consciousness that created it." -Albert Einstein

After my trips to Berlin and Bergamo, I once again felt exhausted, defeated, and back at square one. I was still working crazy hours, going to school at night, and living on minimal rest, so I decided to take a breather and plan a relaxing vacation. At the same time, I had begun to explore brain science and recently discovered an intriguing neurofeedback retreat in France that touted yoga, meditation, and brain-mapping. I decided this new option offered the ideal opportunity to disengage from my everyday life in a serene, peaceful setting devoid of television, internet, alcohol, and the chaos of my everyday life.

After several months of waiting, I was relieved and excited to find myself boarding the plane to Toulouse, France for my new-age retreat adventure. Although I started out with a positive attitude, things changed quickly: I landed in Toulouse late due to flight delays only to discover that the airline also had lost my luggage, and I had no extra clothes or toiletries — just a bookbag full of books. But despite this less-than-ideal start, I decided to go with the flow and boarded my shuttle to the Tourne retreat, which was tucked away in the tiny town of Castelnau Durban at the foot of the French Pyrenees.

After a few hours of driving, the shuttle finally arrived at Tourne and I met the owner of the retreat, Ram Chatlani. Ram manages his own Tao Meditation retreats but opens his cottages to this particular neurofeedback company twice a year. I met my new hosts, Ram, Ram's wife and the couple's young son, and informed them that I did not have any luggage. I asked if I could trouble them for some extra clothing, and they kindly obliged. For a visual reference, I am 5 feet 10 inches tall, so borrowing Ram's petite wife's clothes was not an option; thus I ended up wearing Ram's clothing and shoes and turned out to be quite the sight on my first day there.

The retreat itself was in a lovely, peaceful area devoid of cars, internet, and people. The main house was built of beautiful red marble and surrounded by the vast Forest of Bellissens. Everywhere you looked there was nothing but flowers, trees, nature, complemented by a babbling brook that provided a sense of calm and relaxation. Pleased with my choice, I took a long stroll around while taking in deep breath after deep breath of the clean, crisp mountain air.

I soon learned that there were six other participants at this retreat. We had some brief introductions at dinner and then we were off to bed. My fellow guests included a beautiful young woman from Siberia who had a very serious addiction to social media and her cell phone, an older gentleman from Cannes who never recovered from a serious childhood trauma, and a woman from London who was dealing with PTSD from her abusive husband. They were all lovely people who, much like myself, came here from around the world to confront their own personal demons in search of inner peace.

On our second day we began with a yoga and a meditation session, and then we each had an individual qEEG session. Quantitative EEG Analysis is a type of brain mapping exercise that measures brainwave activity and demonstrates which areas of the brain are overactive or underactive. Scientists and psychologists utilize qEEGs as diagnostics tools to help identify mental health issues like ADHD, PTSD, anxiety and a number of other clinical disorders. Neurofeedback can also be used as a specialized treatment that uses brainwave activity to balance and optimize the brain by teaching it how to self-regulate brain function. Patients who engage in regular brainwave training also report enhanced memory and focus, decreased impulsivity, better mental clarity and improved mood.

I was incredibly excited because I was certain that if I got my brain mapped, then they could tell me from a scientific standpoint what was wrong with me, which would bring me one step closer to being fixed. So I placed the funny-looking electrode helmet on my head, and the team member conducting the exercise inserted some sticky goop in my hair to improve conductivity of the device. She then told me to relax as she opened her laptop and explained that I would be playing a game with my mind while she measured my brainwaves. What I saw in front of me was a 3-D cube; when I was in a relaxed state of mindfulness the cube would remain intact, but when my mind wandered the cube would break apart into pieces. This game went on for about half an hour and overall I thought it was pretty cool that I was playing a videogame with my mind.

A few hours later, the staff sat down with me to discuss my results. They showed me a strange looking piece of paper covered with circles that signified brains, dots that represented brain regions, and sets of differently colored and differently shaped lines. They explained to me that red lines showed areas of overactivity in specific brain regions, while blue lines signified underactivity in other brain regions. Thin lines represented areas of less intense activity, while thicker lines demonstrated more intensity and potential areas of concern. My brainwave activity was compared to clinical research data, and I was informed that my results showed I had an overactive motivation and drive center. Essentially, this meant that I was constantly focused on performing and finding out what's next versus living in the present moment. This brainwave diagnosis explained my inability to calm my mind and inner dialogue. Additionally, I had a lot of activity in my pain centers which predicted that I suffered from anxiety and insomnia — and they were correct.

In addition to the brain mapping, we also had group sessions which I likened to group therapy, but much less formally structured. It was during one of many conversations that I noticed something in particular that the other attendees were doing, a behavior that I had also observed in myself. They were speaking as if they were victims of their past, and as if there was no hope for their future. Literally every thought, action, or future plan was based on or anchored to some past event from which they could not seem to move forward to achieve peaceful resolution.

In between yoga, meditation, and our group and brain mapping sessions, we had the opportunity to rest and relax. The cottage itself was a large, sprawling three-story complex, and on the top floor common area there was a sizable library filled with books from Ram's own collection along with books that had been left behind by his guests over the years. It was like a Barnes and Noble library for self-help; ironically, or perhaps serendipitously, there also happened to be a book in Ram's collection titled *Childhood Disrupted* by Donna Jackson Nakazawa.

Out of the thousands of books there, for some reason Jackson Nakazawa's work called out to me, so I picked it up. This book's overarching premise is that we can become so engrossed in our past that we do not know how to move forward, and we thus make that past a part of our present identity. According to the author, some of us simply believe that we are broken and will be ill for life, and the more you fortify these feedback loops and strengthen the neural connections around the trauma, the more you strengthen and emphasize the victim mentality. The way I read this book was that I had a choice: I could keep strengthening those negative loops, or I could choose to move on, quiet my mind, and start taking responsibility for my choices and my future.

During this retreat week I had many great teachers including several highly knowledgeable staff members from the neurofeedback clinic, but there was no teacher more important and no one I learned more from than Ram. Have you ever met someone and just immediately felt an innate calling to hear their entire life story? Ram was one of those fascinating people: an Englishman and former barrister who led such a high-stress life that he nearly had a heart attack and died while arguing in court. He spoke to me for hours on end about how he felt for years like he was losing his mind, and eventually it got so bad that he wanted to get away from all the chaos and noise. Finally, he got to the point where he was so fed up that he quit his job on a whim and moved his wife and son to the countryside in France. He moved specifically to an area with limited internet and decided to live off the land and run spiritual retreats for people looking to relax and reconnect with themselves and nature.

Almost every element of Ram's life story resonated very deeply with me. He has successfully accomplished the very objective that I had been wandering aimlessly and seeking for years. He found peace with his wife, son, and donkeys in an idyllic French country home and has subsequently devoted his life to helping others find peace. Ram and I had many heartfelt discussions during my stay at Tourne, and he even prescribed some interesting out-of-the-box therapeutic activities, such as telling my troubles to a tree. (You should try this one, trust me.)

No doubt the Tourne retreat was a relaxing escape, but I don't think that having a brain scan is a necessary part of healing. While brain scans can provide insights into human behavioral patterns, ultimately the scan didn't tell me anything I didn't already know, or at least anything that I couldn't figure out on my own if I had been properly in tune and in touch with my body and emotions. If you love brain science as much as I do, then feel free to give it a whirl. You should be able to find someone at a local hospital or research center who can conduct the scan for you, and it is quick and painless. In fact, if you really want to nerd out, you can buy at-home headsets to do brain training in the comfort of your home.

Shortly after I returned home, I emailed Ram and explained that I was not sleeping well and had been very stressed. He sent me the following email and I absolutely loved the simplicity of his advice, so I wanted to share it with my readers:

Ram's Rules for Peace and Happiness:
Ram's Lesson number one: Stop thinking.
Ram's Lesson number two: If you can't stop thinking, don't listen to your thoughts.
Ram's Lesson number three: If you listen, don't believe them.
Ram's Lesson number four: If you believe them, don't believe them for long.
If lessons one to four don't work, go tell your worries to a tree.

If you would like to learn more about the retreats at Tourne, or just would like to absorb more of Ram's wonderful philosophy and life lessons, please visit Tourne.eu. And be sure to tell him that Rachel says hello.

16 PLANT MEDICINES

"Do not blindly believe what others say. See for yourself what brings contentment, clarity, and peace. That is the path for you to follow." -Buddha

When I was at the neurofeedback retreat, there were four primary staff members who assisted specifically with yoga, meditation and administration of the brain scans. On one occasion as I was getting hooked up to the scanning machinery (i.e., the electrodes were being attached to my head), I struck up a conversation with one of the practitioners. It started out with making small talk about where he was from and his past experiences with the retreats, but the conversation soon veered into something strange and unfamiliar to me. He mentioned something called plant medicines, a term I had never heard of before. My interest piqued, I insisted that he share more information with me, but he seemed uncomfortable and quickly tried to change the subject.

He clearly regretted bringing up the topic — as these plant medicines conflicted with the work that we were doing at the retreat, so he could get in trouble for mentioning them. But I promised not to repeat anything he said and convinced him that he could trust me. He told me that he works with a group of individuals in England that specializes in plant medicine retreats, but these retreats were very secretive and you had to be invited by a member. In order to remain elusive, they constantly moved the retreats around the country, never using the same location twice; moreover, each retreat had its own unique combination of topics and medicines.

I had never heard of these medicines before, and obviously I was intrigued. How did they work? What did it cost? Why do people take them? Essentially, he told me that these plants cured numerous mental health disorders, and they helped some people to see God and reach enlightenment. To which I thought to myself, "Shut the front door! Sounds too good to be true." According to this gentleman in front of me, I'll just take some weird plant medicine and the entire world will make sense to me. As open-minded and daring with my treatment as I was to this point, I just had to see for myself.

After begging and pleading to be invited into his group, he caved in and hesitantly provided me with an email address, along with strict instructions to never directly mention any details of the healing regimen when I corresponded with these people. To advertise the events, they used code names like "tea parties" or "mother ceremonies" and I had to exercise the utmost level of discretion. I reached out to the email address given to me, and the only instructions I received in the reply message were a date, an address, a request to bring a sleeping bag, and strongly worded suggestions to fast the day of the ceremony.

Only a few short months after leaving France, I found myself embarking on my next self-improvement adventure. This time I was on a flight to Gatwick Airport, with the final destination being the southern England county of East Sussex. If you have ever flown through Gatwick, then you know that the border protection agents there take their job very seriously. When I landed, they wanted to know the exact address of where I was going, who I was staying with, and why I was going there. Under a barrage of questions I stood there in stunned silence, but I think the dumbfounded look on my face said it all: I literally had no idea what to say. In my mind, the truth sounded even worse than saying nothing: "Some random people I've never met, a house somewhere I have never heard of, and to do some plant medicines. Cool?" They actually took me aside into a private room, where after sweating bullets for 15 minutes I finally gathered enough wits to make up a story that I was staying at a yoga retreat with an unlisted address.

Somewhat miraculously the agents bought my story, and hours later I was finally allowed to leave the airport. I had no idea what I was in store for next; all I knew up to this point was that the ceremony was still on and would begin after dark. I arrived via taxi to the secret address, and I have to say that everything that happened afterward regarding my entire experience was nothing short of surreal. We were all just a bunch of strangers at some random house in the middle of the woods, and I was the only American. I was putting all my trust and faith in these people, because I just wanted to experience what they had all experienced before and I was willing to do anything to get to this level of peace and enlightenment.

There were about 25 of us in total. Four men and women led the ceremony, and the rest of us were participants observing their words and actions and taking their direction. We all set up sleeping bags in a massive living room; I had arrived much earlier in the day than the other guests, and so I was like a kid waiting for their parents to take them to the amusement park. I just sat on my sleeping bag for eight hours asking the leaders, "Are we starting now? What about now? Now?" I was flying blind yet extremely excited, because I was about to be forever enlightened.

Then finally, around 11pm the group leaders told us we were going to begin. They divided men and women to opposite sides of the room and gave us all a bucket, which of course I found odd. They began the first round of the ceremony by providing all of the participants with a sip of a substance called ayahuasca, and they suggested meditating while the "medicine" worked its way through your bloodstream. Excited at the novelty of the process, took my swig of the foul-tasting concoction, and sat on my sleeping bag for what seemed like hours. Then they started the official ceremony, which was full of tribal dancing with feathers, flames and face paint, people screaming and sobbing, and some participants even snorting tobacco up their nose to heighten the effects. It was clear that everyone around me was having some sort of interesting experience, but as for me I was just feeling sick. Not enlightened at all, but rather very, very queasy — so queasy that at one point I thought I was going to explode. Let's just say that this medicine doesn't stay put, and it has to come out one way or another.

One of the guides came over to me and handed me a bucket. She informed me that they throw up together as a group, and doing so was a shared spiritual catharsis. Ahhh, now I understood the purpose of fasting and of the buckets, but to throw up in public in front of a bunch of strangers seemed very uncomfortable to me... so I tried my best to hold it in. The group continued to encourage me to throw up, and they said doing so would make me feel better. Then they asked on more than one occasion if I would like to try tobacco up the nose to facilitate the experience.

The ayahuasca ingestion ceremony has its roots in the ancient traditions of the Inca culture from whence the plant originates, with drums, flames, singing, screaming, and intense emotional outpouring (the tobacco-snorting is probably a modern — and wholly unnecessary — addition). Regardless, at no point in my own personal journey did I feel any enlightening effects, and I just could not get over how weird the experience was. Moreover, I still get nauseous today just thinking about what happened next: in yet another "anything goes" impulsive moment in my winding journey to the holy grail of mental stability, I somehow agreed to the tobacco snort.... and let me tell you, this was NOT fun at all. They used a traditional pipe that shoots tobacco up your nasal cavity, and it burns intensely on the way up the passages, into your eyes and then even out of your ears. Immediately after the tobacco hit, I started to vomit like I have never vomited before... but I had fasted, remember, so I have no clue what in the world I was throwing up. After three separate rounds of drinking ayahuasca and snorting tobacco, I just wanted it all to be over: it was all confusing, disorienting, uncomfortable and not even remotely what I had expected.

After what seemed like an eternity, the sun was finally rising and the effects of the medicine began to wear off for the others in my group. The group leaders graciously and mercifully offered us the option to partake in a meal, and told us to rest. At this point, I was seething and could hardly keep my disappointment from bubbling to the surface. This was certainly not what I had signed up for, and on top of that I had spent the past eight hours feeling as physically ill as I had ever felt in my life. I accepted and wolfed down the meal they provided me (a simple vegan stew) and then promptly passed out in my sleeping bag. Several hours later, I woke up to the excited chatter of the other ceremony participants sharing their experiences of talking to ancestors and seeing God. "What the hell is wrong with me?" I angrily mused. I did exactly what the group leaders told me to do and I saw nothing, I heard nothing, I felt nothing. (Well, except for hunger and nausea.)

Later that day the retreat leaders told us that we were going to switch gears which meant switching "medicines" to achieve another transcendent experience. They were going to hold another ancients-inspired traditional ceremony involving peyote, which I was told was a different plant that helps connect humans to nature. Ever the open-minded experimentalist, and yearning to make up for my ayahuasca experience (or lack thereof), I decided to try my hand at this second ceremony. Well, I must let you know that none of these natural plant medicines taste very good, and peyote specifically is not just figuratively but also quite literally a hard pill to swallow. I gagged down as much of the strange herb as I could handle, then went off into the woods to meditate on my own in hopes of finding magic.

Let's just say this experience was no better than the night before. I sat in the woods for hours feeling nothing but more nausea, then I came back to the campsite to once again find people my retreat colleagues in various enthralled states of bliss. Several were dancing and singing and by their own accounts experiencing utter joy and transcendence. I couldn't believe what I was seeing, mostly because the only effect the peyote had on me was to cause me to wretch and vomit multiple times that night. I departed from the campsite the next morning feeling disgusting: disheveled, shaky, exhausted, and still nauseous. I had paid a significant amount of money to go on this retreat, and of course I was regretting my decision in more ways than just financially. Prior to leaving, I had spoken to the retreat coordinators who explained to me that every so often it takes an individual a few tries at these special plant medicines to experience their acute psychedelic effects. Quite a veteran salesman move, because by hook or by crook I found them talking me into attending another retreat...

Hoping for the third time to be the charm, I opted for a more intense and immersive experience in the woods of Bath, England. The event organizers set up on one of the participant's farms which included a massive teepee in the woods that could sleep about 40 people. This time I was much better packed and prepared for the weekend to come, and more importantly I made a conscious effort to think more positively about my experience in the moment. But alas, long story short: this third experience was even worse than the first two, and laughably so. One of the girls taking the medicine thought she was possessed by a demon and tried to jump into the fire in the middle of the teepee! The entire time I just sat there like I was watching a bad movie, unsurprise and unfazed on account of my two prior disappointing retreats. Chalk up another expensive failure filled with nothing but sickness and vomiting for me.

I approached the event coordinators again, and not surprisingly they yet again assured me that this lack of medicinal effect had never happened before to anyone attending their retreats. They suggested I might need something stronger, so they offered me another plant medicine called Iboga. And again, I had no clue what in the hell this new substance was, but they put me in contact with an "expert" in coordinating Iboga retreats. I was told that Iboga is like ayahuasca on steroids and it works for everyone — results would be guaranteed. I thought about it for a bit (given my track record, I probably spent less time thinking about it than I should have, to be honest) and concluded that the plant medicine route was worth one final try. At this point in time I still believed that I was fundamentally broken and thus clinging onto hope for some sort of quick fix. I also continued to believe the coordinators because everything they said was in alignment with the research I had done on my own. This was their best and final offer, and in my mind it simply HAD to work.

I headed back to England for the very last time in search of en-lightenment. I don't want to relive the gory details of what hap-pened on this fourth excursion, but let's just say it was more of the same: two days of pure hell. Iboga tastes like rotten bark, and the induced vomiting is far more violent than with ayahuasca. It was a smaller group of participants on this retreat, and each and every one of them achieved some sort of colorful insight into their lives whereas I achieved nothing but more sickness and despair. I left from that trip frustrated and discouraged, and more importantly I vowed never to touch any of these plant medicines again.

Although these mind-altering natural substances may sound amazing, and it might be your type of fun to take a little "trip" (pun intended), from my own first-hand experience I advise you to take extreme caution in your approach to experimenting with them. They are not going to have the same magical positive effects for different individuals, and you most certainly should not believe anyone who tells you that you are guaranteed to see God and be enlightened. You should also be aware that you can have a bad trip that can result in you feeling lethargic, depressed or anxious for months afterward. And although some people tout these plant medicines as effective in treating drug addiction, anxiety, depression and PTSD, results from the medical research community remain inconclusive.

If after reading about my experience you still remain interested in exploring plant medicine usage, then find a facility that specializes in these medicines and ensure that they require you to complete a medical background and that they have qualified medical staff onsite. Be aware that you are most likely not going to find such qualified service providers in the United States, and you may have to travel a great distance (i.e,. to Europe or South America). Also, if you do decide to participate, go in with no expectations of what will happen and keep an open mind.

Not surprisingly, I am permanently done with my experimentation on plant medicines. Taking them only made me sick and anxious, and they made me think that there was something wrong with me because I wasn't having the experience that other people were having. I was looking for something that simply didn't exist in my mind, and I was searching for answers in the wrong places. I was looking externally, but it was gradually becoming more clear to me that I needed to start looking within.

Upon returning home and reflecting deeply on these experiences, I finally came to the conclusion that I was not broken, and that the only thing wrong with me was me. I was living in my past, thinking I was condemned to some horrible future unless I found a way to fix myself. But there was nothing that I really needed to fix except my own mindset. I was living in a hell of my own creation, built by and anchored to the experiences of my past. I was blaming others versus creating my own abundant future; I was looking for and waiting for bad things to happen in my life, focusing all my attention on some negative outcome; I was fixated on making my life miserable. And shortly after I returned from my fourth and final trip and failure to launch, I happened to stumble upon this quote from Dr. Joe Dispenza: "Where attention goes, energy flows." It took some time for me to really grasp and internalize that concept, but I knew immediately that it was a very powerful quote and one that eventually led me to my next interesting adventure.

17 DR. JOE

"The one who follows the crowd will usually get no further than the crowd. The one who walks alone, is likely to find himself in places no one has ever been." -Albert Einstein

Even though my last few trips were not the life-changing experiences I was hoping for, they still provided me with some much-needed insight and self-reflection. I started to spend less time worrying about my future and more time planning it; less time trying to fix myself and more time focusing on nurturing my mind, body, and soul. I took vacations to relax instead of trying to find quick-fixes for spiritual enlightenment. It would take a full year, but I finally left my high-stress job in Italy, completely ended an emotionally abusive and toxic relationship, finished my degree, and returned back to the United States to start a brand-new life — a life where I didn't owe anyone anything and I had the freedom to make my own choices, on my own terms, in my own time.

I was living in the Northern Virginia/DC area, working as a consultant for one of the Big Four firms and enjoying my newfound freedom. I was reading and watching literally everything I could get my hands on in regards to spirituality, self-growth, health, and well-being. One day I was watching one of my favorite webcasts, Impact Theory with Tom Bilyeu, and Tom's guest was Dr. Joe Dispenza (aka Dr. Joe). There is a good chance you have already heard of Dr Joe, but for those that haven't, he is a renowned chiropractor who several years ago was in a horrible biking accident that nearly

killed him. Doctors told him that he needed several major surgeries yet it would still be unlikely he would ever heal fully. Dr. Joe
claims he ignored the advice of his doctors and instead focused on
inner healing, which led him to experiencing a full recovery from
his injuries.

Dr. Joe went on to author a series of books and star in several
movies that explained the power we all have within us to heal
our own bodies and create our future. His analysis focuses more
specifically on our thoughts, and he attempts to take a scientific
approach to explaining, and putting into practice, the Law of Attraction. Simply put, the Law of Attraction states that you attract
what you are. If you are negative and spiteful, you will attract
negative and spiteful people and events into your life; conversely,
if you are positive and kind, you will attract into your life positive
and kind people as well as events with positive outcomes.

My interest piqued from Dr. Joe's webcast, so I decided to purchase
his book *The Placebo Effect*. This first work really resonated with
me, so I purchased several more of his books. Then I started his
online workshop which consists of pre-recorded live events and
meditations. Continuing to enjoy his work, I decided to invest in
the next step: a weeklong retreat. If you search the Dr. Joe website,
you will find his retreats are located in some of the most interesting and exotic places in the world. They also all sell out within
five minutes of the registration windows opening, so I reasonably
assumed the retreat offerings were as legitimate as his books and
website. After a little research, I decided I was going to try out
his retreat in Cancun, Mexico. I knew I had previously sworn off
hoaxes and quick fixes, but I figured the worst case scenario here
was that I would meet some positive people in a lovely tropical
location, and the massive amount of meditation over that week
would be good for my mental health.

One very interesting aspect of Dr. Joe's retreats is that they don't
tell you what you are going to do before you get there. I was
working under the assumption that they would follow the for-

mat of the online workshops, which were approximately four to five hours of lectures with some meditations in between. I kept waiting for an agenda, but they said there wasn't one. All I was responsible for was completing the online prep work and showing up on time. So after months of waiting I finally boarded my flight to Cancun excited about this retreat thinking I would spend half the time in lectures and workshops and the other half on the beach getting a tan.

We started Sunday night in the hotel's largest conference room and it was a sight to see, I must say. A thousand people, many of whom were wearing bizarre costumes from unicorns to superheroes, were dancing around in a dark room filled with loud music, flashing lights, glow sticks and disco balls. They were hugging and laughing, and oddly many attendees already seemed to know each other. The moment I walked in, I thought, "Oh God, this is a cult!" and I was the only one who didn't get the memo. I was definitely concerned.

Dr. Joe walked into the room in cult-like leader fashion. He didn't take questions or interact with the audience, and it became apparent there was little chance one would even get to say hello to him the entire time at the retreat, which I found to be incredibly odd. Dr. Joe grabbed the mic and explained that there was no agenda, and that he planned the retreat days on the fly by how he felt. (Interesting, I thought.) He said the week was going to be intense, and that we could forget about lounging on the beach and getting a tan; I was starting to get more and more concerned. Then he dropped the bomb on us: we would be waking up at 3am several times this week to participate in three-to-five-hour long mediations, and a typical workshop day would last anywhere between 10-15 hours. I was on edge at this point and beyond annoyed at what I was hearing.

I went back to my hotel room that night and contemplated what I should do. I was already at this beautiful all-inclusive resort in Cancun so I could just ditch this conference and just go lay on the beach all day and sip tropical cocktails. I begrudgingly decided to go with the flow and see what would transpire, since the conference was extremely expensive and regardless I had been looking forward to trying some longer meditations. I showed up at the assigned predawn hour the next morning, and as we began the format looked and sounded similar to his online workshops. He explained a concept called the quantum and talked about the science behind it, and then we put into practice a meditation. This initial curriculum wasn't too painful and I found myself agreeing with most of what he was saying, which was essentially that we energetically attract to us what we focus on.

I was finally starting to get on board with the Dr. Joe show and settle into a rhythm, when something weird happened. As we started our first mediation, things went downhill fast. People started screaming and crying, and some of the attendees literally fell out of their chairs onto the floor and started writhing around like snakes. "WTF is going on here?" I thought to myself while struggling to keep my cool and focus on my meditation curriculum. Afterward, Dr. Joe explained that these people were "popping" — that is to say, they were entering the quantum and leaving their bodies to enter the fifth dimension. Now I am a very analytical, realistic person who tries to keep an open mind, but when I heard him say this I was completely floored (figuratively, not literally). None of this "popping" concept was mentioned in his books or online workshops. I did not at that instant, and still do not today, buy Dr. Joe's explanation. Moreover, it was somewhat frightening to have people next to you rolling around on the floor like they are having seizures or dying.

As I started to engage at more length with people at the retreat, I realized that a large number of them were taking mind-altering drugs which explained the frequency of the peculiar behavior. The days were getting weirder and weirder, but stubborn little me decided to be a trooper and keep going. Each day we were waking up earlier and earlier and people kept "popping" left and right. But then, something even stranger happened: Dr. Joe claimed at one point that someone in the audience had been spontaneously cured of cancer. Now I was confident that this was a cult, and I wasn't drinking any more of its Kool-Aid and blindly believing its leader.

It was strange enough that he didn't interact with the audience and that he had massive amounts of blind followers frequenting his retreats, but now Dr. Joe was basically likening himself to a deity with the power to heal other humans. As much as my hope-filled heart would have loved to believe this, my scientific rational mind immediately called BS. I do believe that over time we can heal our bodies with the power of positive thinking. But the idea of spontaneous healing exceeds the limits of credibility and has never been scientifically documented (regardless of what Dr. Joe tells his followers, the research does not exist). At this point I said to myself, "Rachel, you met a lot of really nice people and spent many fruitful hours meditating... now go relax on the beach." While I did learn some valuable lessons about focusing my attention and energy on things I want to create in my life, I was not going to listen to anything else Dr. Joe had to say.

Does the fifth dimension exist exactly as Dr. Joe describes it? My personal opinion is that it probably does not. However, I do believe that our thoughts and actions are extremely powerful in attracting people and experiences into our lives. If you focus on fear, hate, sickness and self-loathing, the universe will deliver all of these things to you. If your thoughts focus on happy and positive events and people entering your life, then the Universe does the same. When you focus on being the creator and not the victim of your life, good things come to you. And while life won't be perfect all the time, if you can put negative experiences into perspective and think of them as teaching tools versus punishments, you will slowly start to wake up to a more peaceful and abundant world.

Now when it comes to Dr. Joe, here is my honest recommendation. Watch the Impact Theory webcast and if you like what he has to say, then read *The Placebo Effect*. If this book resonates with you and you want to learn more, then I would recommend his progressive and intensive online workshops. I have found all these resources very valuable and believe he has some great insights into how to manage your mind and maintain an optimistic attitude in the face of hardship or extreme duress. As for the Dr. Joe retreats themselves, they are very expensive and very time-intensive. The weirdness notwithstanding, if you don't cringe at the idea of paying thousands of dollars in workshop, lodging, and travel fees to wake up at 3am for five-plus hour meditation, then this might be the retreat for you. However, I think developing a daily mindfulness and/or meditation routine is far more important, beneficial and realistic.

I would be remiss if I did not warn you that there is a great deal of debate in regards to Dr. Joe, his teachings, and even his legitimacy as a doctor. Most of the research he discusses in his workshops cannot be found in medical journals, and his scientific credentials are not documented. Additionally, he has never released his medical records proving that he was in an accident and/or actually healed himself. Another fundamental problem I have with Dr. Joe is that he expertly understands the power of the subconscious mind and how it is highly impressionable. It doesn't judge between true and false, right and wrong; it just absorbs information constantly even when you are sleeping.

Dr. Joe also understands that when you enter into a deep meditative state such as that achieved in his workshops, you tap into your subconscious mind. If you've already spent 40+ hours on his prep work and videos — and yes, he repeats concepts over and over again during the lessons — what should happen during these mediations is that the subconscious will absorb the information. I believe that a lot of the people at his retreats have the "otherworldly" experiences that they do because Dr. Joe has already imprinted his teachings onto their subconscious faculties. That is my honest opinion and I will leave it to you to decide for yourself, but please be wary if you encounter any retreat that promises magical results or quick fixes because you are likely to come away disappointed.

18 SOMETIMES A BREAK FROM ROUTINE IS THE VERY THING YOU NEED

"Life begins at the end of your comfort zone." -Neale Donald Walsch

After my experiences with sensory deprivation chambers, neurofeedback retreats, plant medicines, traditional and new-age therapies, and Dr. Joe, I was now confident that there was never going to be one "A-ha!" magical moment of insight where I would suddenly become enlightened or instantaneously healed. Instead, I celebrated the little victories like the ability to get a full night's sleep, less thoughts racing through my head, and refinement of an inner voice that focused on the positive people and experiences in my life.

Additionally, I made a promise to myself to take at least two vacations each year. One vacation would be to nurture my relationships with my family and friends, and another one would be to focus on self-development and allow myself to detach from my everyday routine. These trips provide time and space for me to reflect on where I am at physically, emotionally, academically and professionally, and they allow me to celebrate my accomplishments of the past year and strategize new goals for the year to come.

I have traveled to Casablanca and Puglia to practice yoga; Bali to meet with a shaman and explore Indonesia; Lagos to sweat out toxins at a fitness retreat; Sedona to explore energy vortexes; and Bangalore to indulge in an Ayurveda excursion. Instead of spending thousands of dollars puking up tree bark and trying to meditate into the fifth dimension, I have found ways to redirect my time into productive avenues relaxing, reflecting, and experiencing new things apart from my normal routine.

What I have learned time and again is that an essential part of growth is stepping outside of one's comfort zone to attempt novel and different undertakings. I used to live within a tiny, narrow-minded bubble where I tried to control everything possible to avoid anxiety and stress, and all I was doing was making my problems worse by maintaining a stale and confining environment whereby I was squelching and hindering any trial-and-error progression towards true understanding. I now understand that a certain level of discomfort is healthy and that by participating in new and at times frightening growth-related activities, I am stretching and fortifying my brain and developing resilience.

If the idea of stepping outside your comfort zone concerns you, let me counter by delving deeper into the benefits. First, you will be more productive immediately because comfort and complacency destroy productivity. What do you think would happen if your boss or professors never gave you a deadline to finish your work? Expectations and timeframes provide us with a sense of unease and urgency that motivates us to complete tasks. Also, without any sense of discomfort we lose the drive and ambition to learn new things, which can also lead to boredom and depression.[36]

Second, you will soon find it easier to manage and respond to new and unexpected changes. Research professor and author Brene Brown explains that one of the worst things we can do for our mental health is to avoid fear and uncertainty due to a sense of vulnerability.[37] If you take risks and challenge yourself to do things you would not normally do, you can learn to experience some of that uncertainty or fear in a controlled, manageable environment where you can constantly make adjustments to mitigate your anxiety. In fact, when you consciously work to place yourself outside your personal comfort zone on your own terms, you are better prepared for when life's challenges and external forces push you outside it.

Finally, when you strive to explore the space outside your comfort zone, you eventually find that it is easier to brainstorm and harness creativity. When we get into the habit of trying new experiences and learning new skills, we tap into our brain's creative centers that provide inspiration and insights. Trying new things forces us to reflect on our old ideas and memories, so even a positive yet uncomfortable experience will help us to see old problems in a new light. This allows us to tackle future challenges with new perspectives, new insights, and an entirely new state of mind.

If you want to work to expand outside your comfort zone but find yourself with limited funds or resources to do so, don't worry. Keep the goal simple: try to do, see, or eat something new every single day. Trust me, it's not as difficult as it sounds. For example, if you take a daily walk, try taking a different route or stop to speak to a stranger along the way. The next time you go to the grocery store, select a fruit or vegetable you have never eaten before. If you never go to the movies or out to eat alone, give the solo experience a try. Just make an effort to change some aspect of your daily routine, and I promise you will find your brain opening up, evolving and thanking you for its development.

Other next-level suggestions include learning a new skill or language and of course my personal favorite: traveling. Visiting new places and drinking in other cultures is an excellent way to open yourself up to new experiences, broaden your perspectives, and even improve your physical health. One study found that women who travel at least twice a year have a significantly lower risk of suffering from a heart attack than those who travel only once every six years.[38] Traveling has also been proven to dramatically lower stress levels for weeks after a vacation has ended and has been shown to increase cognitive flexibility, depth, and integrativeness of thought.[39] In terms of one's mental health, traveling works to combat depression and enhance happiness and satisfaction.[40]

Once you commit to expanding your boundaries in a systematic manner, you will find that each time you do it becomes progressively easier. Was I ever scared to do it? Absolutely, but every instance where I took a new and unknown step forward, the process became less painful and also has led me to some interesting adventures. For example, a few years ago I was in a hotel lobby for a medical conference in Washington, DC and I randomly found myself conversing with a patent lawyer. I told him I was working on an app to imprint subliminal messages in music and wanted to get his opinion on the patentability of the product. He flat out said not to bother with the app but there was an amazing tech conference every year in Helsinki called Slush, and if I wanted to network with and be inspired by some of the most groundbreaking techies in the world I should consider going.

I had never heard of the conference and I had never been to Finland nor do I speak Finnish, but it looked like an awesome opportunity. I decided to travel to this conference on my own, and I even attended every networking happy hour and free event that they sponsored. At one such event, a woman approached me and asked if I wanted to attend a private poker party. She gave me a card with an address and told me to show up at 8pm sharp. I had no idea what I was getting into but something inside me told me to just say yes. The next thing I knew, I was on a shuttle with a group of tech millionaires to a Venture Capitalist's house on the side of a ski slope right outside Helsinki. They were hosting a Texas Hold 'Em tournament and playing for bitcoin. At that point in time I didn't know how to play cards and wasn't quite sure I understood exactly what bitcoin was, but it ended up being an amazing night where I met some truly exceptional people and made a lot of personal connections. All I did was say yes, which in turn opened myself up to the possibilities of the world.

Our brains crave patterns and routines, which are undeniably important for certain aspects of our lives. However, when we become too rigid in our perspective and approach, we are at risk of becoming inflexible, dulling our senses, and mitigating our adaptability to handle new, challenging situations. When you take the opportunity to pause from your daily routine and push the boundaries of your comfort zone, something magical happens. All the problems you couldn't solve, or issues you didn't know how to approach, the answers will start coming effortlessly to you.

I'd like to challenge you to commit to stepping outside your comfort zone. This could be something big like spending six months hiking in Brazil, or something small like taking the metro to work instead of driving. Or it could mean speaking up and having that uncomfortable conversation with your boss about a promotion or pay raise, because at the end of the day the worst thing they can do is say no to preserve the status quo, but the range of positive outcomes far outpaces the range of negative ones. Remember that every tiny effort you make to experience something different eventually adds up to huge long-term dividends for your personal growth by making you more flexible, more resilient, and more prepared for the next curveball that life will inevitably throw your way.

My personal advice is to actively practice getting uncomfortable and to regularly avoid making decisions based on fear. If a fear of failure is holding you back from taking the leap, or you just need a little extra motivation, I highly recommend watching Charlie Day's Merrimack College commencement address. It's hilarious, heartfelt and inspiring.

19 NEUROSCIENCE FOR DAILY LIFE

You can't cry and do math at the same time. -Scientific Fact

Eldon Taylor, the author of *Subconscious Reprogramming*, wrote one of the most poignant and life-changing quotes that I have ever read: "Shift the focus of change from self to others and what follows incorporates the best of the individual and society at large." I personally interpret this quote as saying that we all have a choice. We can choose to sit around all day trolling social media, complaining about what we are missing, and expressing jealousy that our lives are not as perfect as what we see online. Or we can make the conscious choice to devote our time and energy into something that we are passionate about — more specifically, a passion where you can share your personal gifts with others to help lift them up to their highest potential.

Taylor's quote inspired me to channel my trials and tribulations, adventures, education, and insight into a coaching practice where I help others to improve every aspect of their physical, emotional and cognitive well-being. In my practice, I focus specifically on neurocoaching, a specialized type of coaching where I teach my clients how to approach anxiety, emotions and problem-solving from a state of mindful awareness. I use evidence-based experiential exercises that are shown to produce real-time measurable neurological improvements. I work with my clients to rewire their brains to mitigate stress, anxiety and burnout and in turn improve intuition, insight, communication, empathy, creativity, problem-solving faculties and cognitive performance. And while I can't promise I will take you to the fifth dimension, I can certainly teach you how to effectively manage your mind.

If you are interested in learning more about how you can use brain science to improve your everyday life, then I highly recommend reading *Neurowisdom*. It is written by Mark Waldman, a key mentor of mine and one of the pioneers of this new coaching movement. I first read Mark's book several years ago and loved it so much that I reached out to him directly to learn more about his techniques. *Neurowisdom* teaches key concepts such as the power of gratitude, the science of happiness, techniques to control negative inner speech, and how to navigate painful memories. Waldman presciently teaches us that we have the power to change our neurological past, and the emotions that are associated with it, through practice and patience.

Neurowisdom also explains that to reach any important goal, you need to develop four neurological processes: motivation, decision making, creativity and awareness. And when it comes to achieving these goals, your biggest enemy is stress: "Even brief periods of anxiety, frustration, or ruminating on negative thoughts will interfere with the healthy functioning of neurons in the frontal lobe. In fact, stress causes dendrites (neural receptors in your brain) to dramatically shrink, thereby interfering with every dimension in the decision-making process."[41] This is yet another key reason why I continue to emphasize the importance of mindfulness breaks throughout this book. When you interrupt daily stress with frequent breaks, the dendrites have the ability to recover and grow back, which will help you to avoid burnout.

Understanding neuroscience can also help us to manage difficult emotions. Let's take fear, for example: from a neuroscientific perspective, fear is not a real thing. That does not mean that your feelings are not valid — they definitely are, but we should take a step back and look at it from a different perspective. Our brains are instinctually designed to constantly seek out fear and danger rather than positivity. It's a survival technique rooted in the evolutionary core of our species: what would happen if our ancestors were so enthralled with a lovely butterfly that just flew into their cave that they failed to notice the hungry lion standing behind them?

Every time you enter a new situation, your brain is scanning for potential threats. It is pulling from its bank of past memories to predict which of the many potential outcomes will occur next, and this scanning process is why you experience fear even if there is no danger in the present situation. Thankfully, most modern-day humans no longer need to worry about the threat of an actual lion, but our brains still tend to exhibit laser-like focus onto the negatives in every situation. If you find yourself in a context where you are feeling fearful yet there is no imminent threat, simply take a moment to pause and remind yourself that this is simply your brain predicting what will happen next and that your brain is simply trying to protect you.

One very effective technique I use in neurocoaching is to anchor your mind on value words in those moments when you encounter a nagging or uncomfortable emotion. Anchoring is a valuable tool to help you to remain calm and relaxed so that you can reduce physical stress and mental fatigue and allow the brain to reset, through the release of dopamine. Value words — or to be more specific, your deepest innermost values — provide meaning and purpose in life.

When you have a moment to put down this book, close your eyes and take a few breaths to relax more deeply. When you achieve a state of calm, ask yourself: "What is my deepest innermost value?" Don't try to force the answer with your analytical mind, and if nothing comes to mind don't stress out — you can always try again later. There are an endless number of possibilities for your personal value word; some examples might include connection, honor, trust, love, equity, fairness, respect, and there is no wrong answer. In addition to providing meaning and purpose, value words are effective for the same reason that we as humans cannot do math and cry at the same time. These actions require two separate brain networks that cannot operate simultaneously; in the same token, abstract thinking interrupts negative thoughts and feelings.

You can cry or you can do math, but not both at the same time. No matter how painful that math problem in front of you might be. If you find yourself sobbing uncontrollably over some issue and cannot seem to stop, here's some odd but effective advice: crack open a math book. It might not be fun, but at least you will stop crying. If you don't want to do math, no worries: just try anything that requires abstract thinking like reciting the alphabet backwards, identifying prime numbers, or focusing on your value word. It might seem strange but give it a try. Just repeat your value word to yourself and observe what happens to your mental and physical state. Research shows that by repeating a value word you can instantly decrease stress and anxiety.[42]

If you are struggling with burnout, stress or difficult emotions, or you simply want to improve your cognitive performance, I highly recommend working with a neurocoach. If you are not ready to commit, then give *Neurowisdom* a try. If these techniques and exercises resonate with you early on, then I would highly recommend some of Mark's other books, *Words Can Change Your Brain* and *How Enlightenment Changes Your Brain*. Additionally, *You Are Not Your Brain* by Jeffrey Schwartz, a Research Psychiatrist at UCLA School of Medicine, explains how you can identify negative thoughts and improve bad habits and is another one of my favorite books I tote in my vacation luggage. An understanding of brain science has helped improve my life tremendously, so I highly encourage you to explore how your own brain works... preferably BEFORE you experience a total mental breakdown like I did.

20 RACHEL'S LIFE HACKS

"Life doesn't need to be as difficult as we choose to make it." -Rachel Kozy

A few months ago, I was discussing personality tests with a friend who comes from a very large family. She explained that each of her siblings had taken the Wagner Enneagram Personality Style Scales (WEPSS) assessment to better understand each other's personality styles so they could communicate more effectively with one another. I had completed dozens of personality tests but I had never heard of this one, so I was intrigued and gave WEPSS a spin.

WEPSS identified me as an "Effective Person" and at first I was disappointed that I didn't score higher for traits like loving, wise, or loyal, but after some reflection I embraced my results. Throughout the average day, I am constantly assessing my home, schedule and work environment in search of ways to be more efficient and accomplish more in less time. And I don't want to wrap up this book without sharing a few more of my personal life hacks with you.

Demystifying Meditation

Meditation is a powerful tool that has the ability to help prevent, treat and even cure a plethora of physical and mental ailments ranging from fibromyalgia to depression. If that isn't enough motivation to meditate, consider this: meditation provides the ability to achieve a greater sense of clarity that can increase happiness, health and restfulness while reducing stress. The average human being has approximately 50,000 to 70,000 thoughts every day. I want you to understand that the goal of meditation is not to silence these thoughts. It is simply to detach from them. You can do this by focusing on your breath, reciting a mantra such as "all is well" or "I am not my thoughts," or simply acknowledging your thought and let it drift by without associating any meaning to it.

When we find ourselves constantly succumbing to negative thoughts or feelings, this bad habit can generate heightened stress levels and feelings of hopelessness, isolation, fear and anxiety, not to mention greater physical stress and susceptibility to disease. When you come to understand that you are not your thoughts, you can make drastic changes to every aspect of your physical and mental well-being.

You also need to keep in mind that it is called a meditation *practice* for a reason. I am also not going to sugar-coat it for you: meditation is like any skill in that you have to develop it, hone it and continue to work on it in order to keep it as an effective part of your arsenal. It might be difficult to start your practice, and you will certainly have good days and bad days, but there is no such thing as a bad meditation. For the first six months that I attempted to meditate I would immediately doze off, so I got angry and complained that perhaps meditation wasn't for me. Over time and with a great deal of patience, I eventually finished a five minute meditation and then subsequently a 10-minute meditation. Nowadays, I can sit for up to four hours in a meditative state (not that I do this often, but I can!), so you will have to trust me and trust the process when I tell you that it's possible.

I believe that once we understand the science behind what we are doing we can assign meaning to our actions and achieve better results, so consider the following paragraphs your crash course on the neuroscience of meditation.

Brainwave states

In order to start meditating, it is helpful to have a basic under-standing of brainwave states, and over time you will be able to identify when you enter into each state. Brainwaves are classi-fied based on their amplitude and frequency, and there are five distinct brainwave states: gamma, beta, alpha, theta, and delta. Gamma brainwaves are the fastest frequency and are responsible for heightened perception and cognitive processing. Beta brain-waves are responsible for alert consciousness, arousal, and prob-lem-solving. Next there are alpha brainwaves, which accompany a more focused yet relaxed state that is ideal for creativity and brainstorming. Theta brainwaves are the next lowest and are ideal for achieving a deep meditative state that is connective to one's intuition; delta brainwaves are for deep sleep that facilitates men-tal and physical repair.

On my first go-round I simply fell asleep when I tried to meditate, which was me passing from beta brainwave state into delta brain-wave state. That shift is the equivalent of pulling the emergency brake and taking a car from 60 to 0 mph, and was not ideal for my mental health. And not to worry if this sounds too confusing and complex. It is not difficult to observe brainwave states: every single night of your life when you drift off to sleep, you move from beta, to alpha, to theta, and finally delta.

Best time to meditate

First thing in the morning or right before bed. These are the win-dows where you are less mentally stimulated and can more easily tap into your subconscious mind and theta brainwave states.

Where to meditate

Do not meditate in your bed. On account of the aforementioned law of association, your body will want to drift to sleep. The best option is to find a space where you are removed from your work, pets, children, significant other, etc. Ideally the room should be dark and you should get into a comfortable position, like on the edge of a couch or chair, with your spine straight. Some people prefer to use eye masks to filter out light, but I do not because I find them to be distracting and uncomfortable.

Meditation for Beginners

There are many different ways to meditate; you should experiment and find a way that is enjoyable for you. Remember that if something feels like a chore or is otherwise inconvenient, you will be less likely to make it into a habit.

YouTube offers thousands of different meditations for free; I would recommend experimenting with guided meditations, meditations with chimes, and meditation with music first. Then continue to test meditations until you find a handful that you love. Another option is brainwave entrainment music, a fascinating cutting-edge science where you can entrain your brain into a specific brainwave state through the use of different frequencies (I will discuss this more in the next section). I use these types of meditations when I am feeling overstimulated and I find they help me settle into a meditative state faster.

Calm® and Headspace® are two popular apps that you can use to organize and execute your meditation regimen. Or, you can make it even simpler and just set a timer on your smartphone — start with 30 seconds of meditating and build up longer times with each progressive session. The key is to remain relaxed, keeping a still body and an open mind. You want your body to be immobile and "asleep" while keeping your mind alert and free-flowing. If a thought comes to you, that's fine: simply recognize, acknowledge and detach from it. If you are struggling to let go of thoughts at first, you can simply just focus on your breath.

Scientific research consistently shows that any amount of meditation practiced on a daily basis can have positive health benefits.

And here is some tough love for you: please don't complain to me that you don't have the time. If you have time to brush your teeth every day, then you have time to meditate.

Brainwave Entrainment

If you want help with studying, meditating, or even just improving your mood, the fastest and easiest tool I can recommend is brainwave entrainment. Please do not be intimidated by the complex new-age name: it simply means to entrain, or synchronize, your brain into a certain brainwave frequency or state. To review: delta waves are for dreamless sleep; theta waves are for when your brain is awake but your body is asleep (e.g., meditation); alpha waves are for relaxed concentration; beta waves are for alert focus; and gamma waves are used for information processing and learning. When it comes to studying, there is some debate as to which brainwave state is ideal, but the two states I personally prefer are gamma and alpha. Research shows that gamma waves are supreme for learning new material and memory recall, while alpha waves work best for imagination, learning, memory and visualization.

Brainwave entrainment is a technique that stimulates the brain into a specific state by using sound, light or an electromagnetic field. The pulses from these sounds or devices encourage the brain to align to a particular brainwave frequency (delta, alpha, beta, gamma, or theta). One common type of brainwave entrainment is executed via music using binaural beats. With this technique, the individual plays music through headphones, each ear receiving a different frequency. Physiologically speaking, when your brain hears two different frequencies simultaneously, it perceives or "hears" a third beat and that is the frequency into which your brain entrains. For example, if you play 35Hz in one ear and 30Hz in the other ear, your brain will automatically subtract the two and perceive an auditory beat of 5Hz, which corresponds to a Theta brainwave state. Thus, music is capable of leading your brain into the ideal brainwave state for studying, or meditating, or motivation, relaxing, sleeping, power napping, etc. (the possibilities are endless).

There are multiple devices available for purchase online, but I would recommend starting with music to determine if this is an effective technique for you. I have included several examples on my YouTube channel, but you can do your own search with the following keywords: binaural beats for concentration and focus, brainwave entrainment for studying, cognition enhancer, and alpha/gamma brainwave states. I recommend experimenting with all different types of music until you find something you find appealing. Before you start, take a deep breath, relax... and be sure to give yourself 10-15 minutes to immerse yourself in the music.

MindZoom

MindZoom is a software that utilizes the power of the subconscious mind to reprogram one's thoughts via subliminal messages. The software offers three features: an affirmation delivering engine, a set of silent subliminal messages, and a subliminal mixer. The affirmation engine conveys thousands of positive words and commands that bypass your conscious mind by rapidly flashing on your computer screen at virtually undetectable speeds. MindZoom's silent subliminal messaging system converts text affirmations to speech and delivers them to the user's subconscious at frequencies not heard by the human ear. Finally, the subliminal mixer allows you to mix text or audio affirmations with your favorite music so you can listen to them anywhere.

Now that I've captured your attention — or perhaps utterly confused you — let's dive into a little background history and context. Subliminal theory started back in the early 1900s with whisper therapy, a medical practice where doctors whispered suggestions to patients in hopes of subconsciously persuading them to improve behaviors.[43] Over time, subliminal messages were embedded into images, music, and sound. Marketing firms have been aware of their ability to influence behavior for almost a century, and one of the first recorded abuses was in the 1943 animated short featuring Daffy Duck where the words "BUY BONDS" appeared briefly on screen.[44] If you would like to learn more about exploitation of subliminal messages, I highly recommend the book *Mind Programming: From Persuasion and Brainwashing, to Self-Help and Practical Metaphysics* by Eldon Taylor. However, I digress and so I will return my focus to how you can capitalize on this science for your own benefit.

In the earlier chapter where I discussed the Dr. Joe retreat, I mentioned how the subconscious mind is highly impressionable, it never turns off, and it accepts all commands without questioning them (i.e., it cannot differentiate between good/bad or right/wrong). This is exactly how subliminal messages work: any suggestions delivered at an inaudible or invisible level will enter directly into the subconscious mind, a phenomenon to which humans are exposed as early as when we are in our mother's womb. MindZoom specifically works to improve negative thoughts and behaviors by replacing them with positive ones in an imperceptible and repetitive way. And according to the MindZoom website, this software can be used to motivate, to learn another language, to remove addictions, and to improve one's mindset. However, please bear in mind that subliminal messages are NOT a panacea or brainwashing device — they work to help improve your motivation and mindset, but ultimately it's up to you to take concrete actions to achieve the personal improvement you seek.

I have been using MindZoom for years and adore this software. I turn on the affirmation engine each morning when I power up my laptop, and my personal affirmations and goals flood my subconscious while I answer emails or catch up on work. I also use the MindZoom subliminal mixer to record my personal messages and embed them into my workout and sleep music. If you don't want to invest in this software but you are interested in experimenting with subliminal music, you can find online and download for free a plethora of effective recordings. Subliminals have been extremely helpful in keeping me positive, motivated and focused on my goals; I believe that they can have the same beneficial effects for you.

Mind Movies®

Think of Mind Movies® as a digital video vision board where you can create your ideal future complete with positive affirmations, inspiring images and motivating music. These short videos utilize the power of visualization to prime your mind for manifestation and inspire you to live your best life. Visualization, or the mental process of imagining a goal or desire in a way that feels more like reality than fantasy, is a technique used by CEOs, professional athletes, and anyone seeking peak performance. Similar to subliminals, visualization works to harness the power of your subconscious mind while reprogramming you for greater self-confidence, positivity, and creativity, all while working to remove emotional or mental blocks that may be detrimental to your success.

It is actually easier than you might think to influence and train your mind for success, due to an interesting area of the brain referred to as the Reticular Activating System (RAS). The RAS consists of a bundle of nerves at the brainstem that receives input from the spinal cord, sensory pathways, thalamus and cortex.[45] Its primary objective is to filter out unnecessary input, and its presence and observed function explains how humans can sort through millions of data points at any given instant in time. The RAS is the reason why once you have decided that you want and absolutely must have a blue BMW, you strangely start to see that exact same car everywhere you look. It filters the world though your given parameters based on your preset beliefs, and then it will focus on whatever you believe and feel you deserve without any conscious effort. By continually flooding your subconscious mind with images of your goals, you can program your RAS to automatically scan your environment in search of solutions to fulfill these desires.

I personally struggle with visualization, so I have found that Mind Movies are an excellent way for me to design my ideal future and program my RAS. I love that the platform is entirely online and easy to use. They offer an extensive library of powerful affirmations, uplifting music, and inspiring digital media clips, or you can upload your own custom content and get really creative in crafting your future. So go ahead, photoshop yourself arm-in-arm with Ryan Reynolds (sorry Blake) at the Academy Awards and sipping cocktails at your pool in your 20 million dollar mansion in the Hollywood Hills, because the sky's the limit. I incorporate my own personal movie into my morning routine to prime my brain for the day, setting a positive short-term mindset alongside reminders to focus on long-term future goals. I am probably on my 20th version of my movie, and believe it's an effective and wildly entertaining tool for goal setting, motivation and peace of mind.

Unwavering Optimism

This last tool is incredibly powerful, and it's one of my favorites. Martin Seligman, a psychologist famous for his work in positive thinking and well-being, teaches that you have to ingrain optimism into your brain "through the power of nonnegative thinking."[46] I have purposely and carefully mentioned several times throughout this book that you control your thoughts, not what they are but how you react to them. I don't do this to be redundant, I do this because I am trying to reprogram your subconscious, and consistency and repetition is key to that reprogramming.

When you are mindfully engaged and aware of your current state of being, you are able to consciously identify and subsequently ignore negative ideas, emotions and beliefs that have been involuntarily stored into your long-term memory. Over time and with patience and practice, you can work to reprogram your brain from a negative pessimistic perspective into a perspective of optimism, joy, and happiness. Research also shows that consciously practicing optimism also dramatically reduces self-doubt, anxiety and depression.[47] When it comes to your career, studies show that optimism leads to increased income and work performance.[48] And when you maintain an optimistic attitude, your motivation and creativity increase and your work becomes more pleasurable.[49,50]

Remember that your mind is in a constant battle with itself. On one side you have your right frontal lobe, the eternal pessimist on constant search for the negative in every situation in order to protect you. On the other you have your left frontal lobe, working overtime to counteract the negativity of your right lobe by searching for creative solutions to attain your goals. These two lobes are constantly flooding your brain with positive and negative thoughts that influence your emotions, mood, and actions. The key is in finding the balance within the tug-of-war by consciously assessing problems with your right lobe and then switching your awareness to your left lobe to search for creative, positive solutions to analyze and solve your problems to bring you one step closer to your goals.

21 FINAL
THOUGHTS

"You can't connect the dots looking forward; you can only connect them looking backwards. So you have to trust that the dots will somehow connect in your future." -Steve Jobs

So here we are, nearly a decade after that fateful trip to Santorini where my body shut down, my mouth involuntarily spewed verbal vomit and I melted into a shell of a human being. It's been quite an adventure since that fateful day, and while it hasn't been a perfect journey I can confidently say that I stand here before you feeling like an entirely new person. Do I have all the answers to life's questions? No, of course not. Will I have another mental breakdown in the future? I'm not rooting for it, but never say never. But if I do, I will be armed with the knowledge, insight and wisdom necessary to bounce back more quickly.

My breakdown inspired me to become the scientist of my life and to educate myself on what my body and brain need to function properly. It taught me about the importance of self-care and of making my own physical and emotional needs my number one priority. I now understand that it's my responsibility to decide how I spend my time, who I spend it with, and how I communicate what I need to those around me. I recognize that my suffering was self-induced and that no amount of money, travel or plant medicines was going to fix me, and more importantly that I can no longer hold onto the past nor blame anyone else but me for my circumstances.

I have learned to make space. So, when the universe sends a tragic blow my way in the form of a heart-wrenching breakup or a humiliating dismissal from an employment position, I have the insight to understand that these are gifts in my life that were sent to make room for something better. And over time, I know I will have the clarity to finally see what these things actually were: a toxic relationship and a dead-end job I dreaded going to every day. Therefore, I now work to not force any outcome, and I firmly believe that disappointment is an indicator that what I desire is not quite ready for me yet. Everything happens exactly when and how it should, and in the meantime I have everything I need inside of me. But most importantly, my breakdown taught me that sometimes the answer lies in not having an answer.

Additionally, gaining a deeper understanding of brain science has provided me a tremendous amount of relief and has taught me how to manage my mind. Recall that the average person has 50,000 to 70,000 thoughts a day; what is the general overall quality of those thousands of thoughts that fill your mind? Are they kind and encouraging and are they moving you in the direction of your ideal life? Or are they hesitant and pessimistic, placing you in a state of constant fear, anxiety, and worry? You have the ability to redirect your thoughts by allowing the negative ones to float by your awareness without assigning meaning to them. You are not your thoughts so focus your time, attention and energy on things in your life that want to manifest and not what you wish to avoid. And don't ever forget that you are the author of your story and you have the power to write any story that you want.

Alas, you might be wondering if I wake up as a ray of sunshine and jump out of bed with a smile every single day. The answer: Hell no! In fact, while writing this book I have stirred up a lot of negative memories and emotions, and today I woke up feeling horrible and like an imposter. Next, I felt bad for feeling bad. But then I took a deep breath, told the right side of my brain to shut the hell up, got my ass out of bed and put one front in front of the other. I have to continually remind myself, on good days and bad alike, that my mind wants to focus on what's wrong but that I have the ability to shift that focus to something more positive. I can meditate or listen to or read something motivational; I can use brainwave entrainment to release endorphins; I can clear my mind with a long cycle in the sun; I can watch my ideal life on my Mind Movie®; I can do some math problems if I start to cry for no reason (although this is the least likely option for me). I have a wide-ranging toolkit of resources at my disposal whenever a negative or uncomfortable emotion starts to surface, and my goal as a first-time author is to share these tools and resources with you.

You could spend an entire lifetime studying each of the topics mentioned herein, so I would suggest using this book as a starting point for you to evaluate your current physical, mental and emotional states. Give yourself credit for areas where you are doing well and perhaps overachieving and identify other areas where you might be struggling. When applying my tools, you might love some and hate others — that's perfectly fine and to be expected. I encourage you to use trial-and-error to determine what works for you and your unique situation, and call "BS" on anyone who tries to tell you how to think, believe or feel.

I want to thank you for letting me share my story. I mentioned before that it's been challenging to relive a lot of these experiences, but it's also been very healing. For that, I am deeply grateful to all my readers. I sincerely hope this book brought you some joy, that you found it relatable, and that I provided you with resources and wisdom to apply to your own life. I'll close with these sentiments: YOU are unique. YOU are loved. YOU are stronger than you realize. Everything that you need is within YOU.

REFERENCES

1. Selhub, E., MD. (2015, November 16). Nutritional psychiatry: Your brain on food [Web log post]. *Harvard Health Publishing.*
2. Knüppel, A., Shipley, M. J., Llewellyn, C. H., & Brunner, E. J. (2017). Sugar intake from sweet food and beverages, common mental disorder and depression: prospective findings from the Whitehall II study. *Scientific reports,* 7(1), 6287.
3. Fothergill, E., et.al. (2016). Persistent metabolic adaptation 6 years after "The Biggest Loser" Competition. *Obesity.*
4. Faris MA, Kacimi S, Al-Kurd RA, Fararjeh MA, Bustanji YK, Mohammad MK, Salem ML. Intermittent fasting during Ramadan attenuates proinflammatory cytokines and immune cells in healthy subjects. Nutr Res. 2012 Dec;32(12):947-55.
5. Sharma, A., Madaan, V., & Petty, F. D. (2006). Exercise for mental health. *Primary care companion to the Journal of clinical psychiatry,* 8(2),106.
6. Suni, E. (2020, December 4). How Sleep Deprivation Affects Your Heart. Sleep Foundation.
7. Jiang, K. (2020, June 4). Fruit Fly Study Reveals Gut's Role In Causing Death by Sleep Deprivation. The Harvard Gazette.
8. Fitzgerald, T., & Vietri, J. (2015). Residual Effects of Sleep Medications Are Commonly Reported and Associated with Impaired Patient-Reported Outcomes among Insomnia Patients in the United States. *Sleep disorders,* 2015, 607148.
9. Durlach J, Pagès N, Bac P, Bara M, Guiet-Bara A. Bio-

rhythms and possible central regulation of magnesium status, phototherapy, darkness therapy and chrono-pathological forms of magnesium depletion. Magnes Res. 2002 Mar;15(1-2):49-66.

10. Sarafoleanu, C., Mella, C., Georgescu, M., & Perederco, C. (2009). The importance of the olfactory sense in the human behavior and evolution. *Journal of Medicine and Life*, *2*(2), 196–198.

11. Lippelt DP, Hommel B, Colzato LS. (2014, September 23). Focused attention, open monitoring, and loving kind-ness meditation: effects on attention, conflict monitor-ing, and creativity - A review. Front Psychol. 23;5:1083.

12. Macit, H , Macit, G , Güngör, O . (2018). A Research on Social Media Addiction and Dopamine Driven Feedback. Mehmet Akif Ersoy Üniversitesi İktisadi ve İdari Bilimler Fakültesi Dergisi. 5(3), 882-897.

13. Pantic I. (2014). Online social networking and mental health. *Cyberpsychology, behavior and social networking*, *17*(10), 652–657.

14. Walusinski O. (2014) How yawning switches the de-fault-mode network to the attentional network by activating the cerebrospinal fluid flow. Clin Anat. Mar;27(2):201-9.

15. Gupta, S., & Mittal, S. (2013). Yawning and its physio-logical significance. *International Journal of Applied & Basic Medical Research*, *3*(1), 11–15.

16. Loucks E, Gilman S, Britton W, Gutman R, Eaton C, Buka S. Associations of Mindfulness with Glucose Regulation and Diabetes. *American Journal of Health Behavior*. 2016.

17. Sundquist J, Lilja A, Palmer K, Memon A, Wang X, Jo-hansson L. "Mindfulness group therapy in primary care patients with depression, anxiety and stress and adjust-ment disorders: randomized controlled trial." *The British Journal of Psychiatry*, 2014.

18. Petersen, A. (2020, February 9). The Surprising Science Behind Friendship. *The Wall Street Journal*.

19. Mineo, L. (2017, April 11). Good Genes are Nice, but Joy is Better. *The Harvard Gazette.*

20. Schoenborn, Charlotte A. "Marital Status and Health: United States, 1999-2002." Advance Data, no. 351, December 2004.

21. Victoria State Government (2017, October 2). Strong Relationships, Strong Health. Department of Health.

22. Kiecolt-Glaser JK, Loving TJ, Stowell JR, Malarkey WB, Lemeshow S, Dickinson SL, Glaser R. (2005). Hostile marital interactions, proinflammatory cytokine production, and wound healing. Arch Gen Psychiatry. Dec;62(12):1377-84.

23. Strubel J, Petrie TA. Love me Tinder: Body image and psychosocial functioning among men and women. Body Image. 2017 Jun;21:34-38.

24. Strubel, J., & Petrie, T. (2016, August 4). Tinder:Swiping Self Esteem? American Psychological Association.

25. Finkel EJ, Eastwick PW, Karney BR, Reis HT, Sprecher S. Online Dating: A Critical Analysis from the Perspective of Psychological Science. Psychol Sci Public Interest. 2012 Jan;13(1):3-66.

26. Jacobson, S. (2015, March 2015). The Psychological Cost of Never Saying No. Harley Therapy Counselling Blog.

27. Schrader, J. (2018, September 11). Why Is It So Hard to Set Boundaries? Psychology Today.

28. The Hague Psychologist. (2016, September 6). What is Blame-Shifting? Escaping Responsibility. Diagnosis.

29. Golden, B. (2018, November 10). 7 Consequences of Blaming Others for How We Manage Anger. Psychology Today.

30. Alberini CM, Ledoux JE. Memory reconsolidation. Curr Biol. 2013 Sep 9;23(17):R746-50.

31. Arntz, A., & Weetrman, A. (1999). Treatment of childhood memories: theories and practice. Behav Res Ther. Aug;37(8):715-40.

32. Anderson MC, Huddleston E. Towards a cognitive and

neurobiological model of motivated forgetting. Nebr Symp Motiv. 2012;58:53-120.

33. Herbert, M. (2018, December 14). Resilience. How Stress Affects Your Body and Brain. Nuffield Health.

34. Santos-Longhurst, A. (2020, April 13). Everything You Need to Know about Sensory Deprivation Tank Therapy. Healthline.

35. Swaminathan R. (2003). Magnesium metabolism and its disorders. *The Clinical biochemist. Reviews, 24*(2), 47–66.

36. Soskin DP, Holt DJ, Sacco GR, Fava M. Incentive salience: novel treatment strategies for major depression. CNS Spectr. 2013 Dec;18(6):307-14.

37. Brown, B. (2013). *Daring greatly: How the courage to be vulnerable transforms the way we live, love, parent and lead.* New York: Penguin Random House.

38. Global Coalition on Aging. (2013, December). Journey to Healthy Aging. Transamerica Center for Retirement Studies.

39. Frédéric C. Godart, William W. Maddux, Andrew V. Shipilov, and Adam D. Galinsky, 2015: *Fashion with a Foreign Flair: Professional Experiences Abroad Facilitate the Creative Innovations of Organizations. AMJ, 58,* 195–220.

40. Kumar A, Killingsworth MA, Gilovich T. Waiting for Merlot: Anticipatory Consumption of Experiential and Material Purchases. *Psychological Science.* 2014;25(10):1924-1931.

41. Waldman, M., & Manning, C. (2017). *NeuroWisdom: The New Brain Science of Money, Happiness, and Success.* New York: Diversion Books.

42. Manning, C. et.al. (2013). Personal Inner Values. A Key to Effective Face-to-Face Business Communication. Journal of Executive Education (1):37-65.

43. Moss, M. (2014, July 23). Probing Question: What is Whisper Therapy. Penn State News.

44. Stern,V. (2015, September 1). A Short History of the Rise, Fall, and Rise of Subliminal Messaging. Scientific American Mind.

45. Arguinchona JH, Tadi P. Neuroanatomy, Reticular Activating System. [Updated 2020 Jul 31]. In: StatPearls [Internet]. Treasure Island (FL): StatPearls Publishing.

46. Seligman M (1997). Learned Optimism. New York: Free Press.

47. Sin, N.L. & Lyubomirsky, S (2009). Enhancing well-being and alleviating depressive symptoms with positive psychology interventions: a practice-friendly meta-analysis. J Clinical Psychol. May;65(5):467-87.

48. Carver, C.S., Scheier, M.F., & Segerstrom, S.C. (2010). Optimism. Clin Psychol Rev. Nov;30(7)879-89.

49. Berridge, K.C. (2007). The debate over dopamine's role in reward: the case for incentive salience. Psychopharmacology. Apr;191(3):391-431.

50. Flaherty, A.W. (2005). Frontotemporal and dopaminergic control of idea generation and creative drive. Comp Neurol. Dec 5;493(1):147-53.

ACKNOWLEDGEMENTS

I would like to thank Carolyn Flower of Oxygen Publishing Agency Inc. for her encouragement in embarking on this massive endeavor and to Alix Sternberg for her help in content development. I also want to give an enormous thank you to my editor, Alvie Loreto, for working your magic and helping to bring my story to life.

ABOUT THE AUTHOR

Rachel Kozy

After decades of suffering from anxiety, insomnia, and depression, Rachel Kozy devoted her life to studying human physiology, cognitive neuroscience, bioenergetics and public health in search of answers. Her passion is helping her clients improve every aspect of their physical, cognitive and emotional wellbeing through her NeuroCoaching practice.

Prior to coaching, Rachel served the US Navy as a Healthcare Administrator and she also has extensive teaching, medical research, startup, and consulting experience. Additionally, she was selected as a Veterans in Global Leadership and Focus Forward fellow, and an Aspen Institute Socrates Scholar. Rachel is the founder of the Empowered Women Brunch, which connects and inspires individuals who are investing in enhancing their personal and professional lives. Additionally, Rachel volunteers with Veterati and American Corporate Partners to provide one-on-one mentoring and guidance to military members who are either transitioning or struggling to find meaningful work. She also serves on the Board of Directors for Lyrica Classic, a global non-profit that allows undiscovered music to find the recognition it deserves.

Rachel is committed to a lifetime of learning and will be joining the Neuroimaging and Informatics program at USC's Keck School of Medicine in the Fall of 2021, and future plans include a PhD in Neuroscience. You can learn more about Rachel and her NeuroCoaching practice at RachelKozy.com.

Made in the USA
Columbia, SC
08 July 2021